ROMEO AND JULIET

ROMEO AND JULIET

WILLIAM SHAKESPEARE

Illustrated by
WILLIAM HATHERELL

LEOPARD

This edition published in Great Britain
in 1995 by Leopard Books,
Random House, 20 Vauxhall Bridge Road,
London SW1V 2SA

Published in the USA
in 1993 by Gramercy Books

Preface and Compilation
Copyright © 1990 by Random House Value Publishing, Inc.
All rights reserved

Grateful acknowledgement is made to
George Weidenfeld & Nicholson Ltd,
for permission to reprint the text used in this edition,
originally published in
The New Temple Shakespeare series,
edited by M. R. Ridley.

Designed by Jean Krulis

ISBN 0 7529 0097 8

Printed and bound in Singapore

8 7 6 5 4 3 2 1

PREFACE

Romeo and Juliet, the haunting story of star-crossed lovers, was written by William Shakespeare when he was only thirty-one years old. He based this simple and moving play on a poem by Arthur Brooke, which, in turn, was taken from a romance by Bandello. A lyrical tale of young lovers doomed to separation and premature death by a family feud and by fate, *Romeo and Juliet* is the quintessential love story.

Shakespeare's plays were first published individually, in Quarto editions. Later they were collected and published in Folio editions. There are often variations in the text from edition to edition. The text of this edition of *Romeo and Juliet* is the nearest possible approximation to what Shakespeare actually wrote and is based on the earliest reliable printed texts. To avoid distraction, however, the spelling has been modernized. Where a Quarto text exists as well as the First Folio, the passages which occur only in the Quarto are enclosed in square brackets and those which occur only in the Folio are enclosed in brace brackets. The punctuation adheres closely to the Elizabethan punctuation of the early texts and, therefore, is often indicative of the way in which the lines are to be delivered.

The wonderful illustrations were done by William Hatherell, who was an important Edwardian landscape and figure painter as well as an eminent illustrator. Hatherell worked, whenever possible, from life and always took great care to reflect accurately both place and period. His magical illustrations for *Romeo and Juliet* depict in startling detail the beauty and the tragedy of this marvellous play, delineate the characters, and capture the passion and the fragility of young love.

This beautiful edition of *Romeo and Juliet*, one of the greatest love stories ever written, is sure to captivate anyone who has ever been in love.

GAIL HARVEY

New York
1990

DRAMATIS PERSONAE

ESCALUS, *prince of Verona.*
PARIS, *a young nobleman, kinsman to the prince.*
MONTAGUE,
CAPULET, } *heads of two houses at variance with each other.*
An old man, of the Capulet family.
ROMEO, *son to Montague.*
MERCUTIO, *kinsman to the prince, and friend to Romeo.*
BENVOLIO, *nephew to Montague, and friend to Romeo.*
TYBALT, *nephew to Lady Capulet.*
FRIAR LAURENCE, *a Franciscan.*
FRIAR JOHN, *of the same order.*
BALTHASAR, *servant to Romeo.*
SAMPSON,
GREGORY, } *servants to Capulet.*
PETER, *servant to Juliet's nurse.*
ABRAHAM, *servant to Montague.*
An Apothecary.
Three Musicians.
Page to Paris; another Page; an Officer.

LADY MONTAGUE, *wife to Montague.*
LADY CAPULET, *wife to Capulet.*
JULIET, *daughter to Capulet.*
Nurse to Juliet.

Citizens of Verona; kinsfolk of both houses; Maskers,
Guards, Watchmen, and Attendants.

Chorus.

SCENE: *Verona; Mantua.*

The Prologue

Enter Chorus

Chorus. Two households, both alike in dignity,
    (In fair Verona, where we lay our scene)
From ancient grudge break to new mutiny,
    Where civil blood makes civil hands unclean:
From forth the fatal loins of these two foes
    A pair of star-cross'd lovers take their life;
Whose misadventur'd piteous overthrows
    Do with their death bury their parents' strife.
The fearful passage of their death-mark'd love,
    And the continuance of their parents' rage,
Which but their children's end nought could remove,
    Is now the two hours' traffic of our stage;
The which if you with patient ears attend,
What here shall miss, our toil shall strive to mend.

ACT I

Scene I

Streets in Verona

*Enter Sampson and Gregory, of the house of Capulet,
with swords and bucklers*

Sampson. Gregory, on my word, we'll not carry coals.

Gregory. No, for then we should be colliers.

Sampson. I mean, an we be in choler, we'll draw.

Gregory. Ay, while you live, draw your neck out o' the collar.

Sampson. I strike quickly, being mov'd.

Gregory. But thou art not quickly mov'd to strike.

Sampson. A dog of the house of Montague moves me.

Gregory. To move is to stir, and to be valiant is to stand: therefore, if thou art mov'd, thou runn'st away.

Sampson. A dog of that house shall move me to stand: I will take the wall of any man or maid of Montague's.

Gregory. That shows thee a weak slave, for the weakest goes to the wall.

Sampson. 'Tis true; and therefore women, being the weaker vessels, are ever thrust to the wall: therefore I will push Montague's men from .the wall, and thrust his maids to the wall.

Gregory. The quarrel is between our masters and us their men.

Sampson. Tis all one, I will show myself a tyrant: when I have fought with the men, I will be civil with the maids; I will cut off their heads.

Gregory. The heads of the maids?

Sampson. Ay, the heads of the maids, or their maiden heads, take it in what sense thou wilt.

Gregory. They must take it in sense that feel it.

Sampson. Me they shall feel while I am able to stand, and 'tis known I am a pretty piece of flesh.

Gregory. 'Tis well thou art not fish; if thou hadst, thou hadst been poor John. Draw thy tool; here comes two of the house of Montagues.

Enter Abraham and Balthasar

Sampson. My naked weapon is out, quarrel, I will back thee.

Gregory. How, turn thy back and run?

Sampson. Fear me not.

Gregory. No, marry; I fear thee!

Sampson. Let us take the law of our sides, let them begin.

Gregory. I will frown as I pass by, and let them take it as they list.

Sampson. Nay, as they dare. I will bite my thumb at them; which is a disgrace to them, if they bear it.

Abraham. Do you bite your thumb at us, sir?

Sampson. I do bite my thumb, sir.

Abraham. Do you bite your thumb at us, sir?

Sampson. (*aside to Gregory*) Is the law of our side, if I say ay?

Gregory. No.

Sampson. No, sir, I do not bite my thumb at you, sir, but I bite my thumb, sir.

Gregory. Do you quarrel, sir?

Abraham. Quarrel, sir? no, sir.

Sampson. But if you do, sir, I am for you: I serve as good a man as you.

Abraham. No better.

Sampson. Well, sir.

Enter Benvolio

Gregory. (*aside to Sampson*) Say 'better,' here comes one of my master's kinsmen.

{*Sampson.* Yes, better, sir.

Abraham. You lie.

Sampson. Draw, if you be men. Gregory, remember thy swashing blow. *They fight*

Benvolio. Part, fools!   *Beating down their weapons*
  Put up your swords, you know not what you do.

Enter Tybalt

Tybalt. What, art thou drawn among these heartless hinds?
  Turn thee, Benvolio, look upon thy death.
Benvolio. I do but keep the peace: put up thy sword,
  Or manage it to part these men with me.
Tybalt. What, drawn, and talk of peace? I hate the word,
  As I hate hell, all Montagues, and thee:
  Have at thee, coward!   *They fight*

Enter several of both houses, who join the fray; then enter
Citizens and Peace-officers, with clubs

First Off. Clubs, bills, and partisans! strike! beat them
    down!
  Down with the Capulets! down with the Montagues!

Enter old Capulet in his gown, and Lady Capulet

Capulet. What noise is this? Give me my long sword, ho!
Lady Capulet. A crutch, a crutch! why call you for a sword?
Capulet. My sword, I say! Old Montague is come,
  And flourishes his blade in spite of me.

Enter old Montague and Lady Montague

Montague. Thou villain Capulet!—Hold me not, let me go.
Lady Montague. Thou shalt not stir one foot to seek a foe.}

Enter Prince Escalus, with his train

Escalus. Rebellious subjects, enemies to peace,
  {Profaners of this neighbour-stained steel,—
  Will they not hear? What, ho! you men, you beasts,
  That quench the fire of your pernicious rage
  With purple fountains issuing from your veins,}
  On pain of torture, from those bloody hands
  Throw your mistemper'd weapons to the ground,
  {And hear the sentence of your moved prince.}
  Three civil brawls, bred of an airy word,

By thee, old Capulet, and Montague,
Have thrice disturb'd the quiet of our streets,
{And made Verona's ancient citizens
Cast by their grave beseeming ornaments,
To wield old partisans, in hands as old,
Canker'd with peace, to part your canker'd hate:}
If ever you disturb our streets again,
Your lives shall pay the forfeit of the peace.
For this time, all the rest depart away:
You, Capulet, shall go along with me;
And, Montague, come you this afternoon,
To know our farther pleasure in this case,
To old Free-town, our common judgement-place.
Once more, on pain of death, all men depart.

Exeunt all but Montague, Lady Montague,
and Benvolio

Montague. Who set this ancient quarrel new abroach?
    Speak, nephew, were you by when it began?
Benvolio. Here were the servants of your adversary
    And yours close fighting ere I did approach:
    {I drew to part them: in the instant came
    The fiery Tybalt, with his sword prepar'd;
    Which, as he breathed defiance to my ears,
    He swung about his head, and cut the winds,
    Who, nothing hurt withal, hiss'd him in scorn:
    While we were interchanging thrusts and blows,
    Came more and more, and fought on part and part,
    Till the prince came, who parted either part.}
Lady Montague. O, where is Romeo? saw you him to-day?
    Right glad I am he was not at this fray.
Benvolio. Madam, an hour before the worshipp'd sun
    Peer'd forth the golden window of the east,
    A troubled mind drave me to walk abroad;
    Where, underneath the grove of sycamore
    That westward rooteth from the city's side,
    So early walking did I see your son:
    Towards him I made; but he was ware of me,
    And stole into the covert of the wood:

I, measuring his affections by my own,
Which then most sought where most might not be found,
Being one too many by my weary self,
Pursued my humour, not pursuing his,
And gladly shunn'd who gladly fled from me.
Montague. {Many a morning hath he there been seen,
With tears augmenting the fresh morning's dew,
Adding to clouds more clouds with his deep sighs:
But all so soon as the all-cheering sun
Should in the farthest east begin to draw
The shady curtains from Aurora's bed,
Away from light steals home my heavy son,
And private in his chamber pens himself,
Shuts up his windows, locks fair daylight out,
And makes himself an artificial night:}
Black and portentous must this humour prove,
Unless good counsel may the cause remove.
Benvolio. My noble uncle, do you know the cause?
Montague. I neither know it nor can learn of him.
{*Benvolio.* Have you importun'd him by any means?
Montague. Both by myself and many other friends:
But he, his own affections' counsellor,
Is to himself—I will not say how true—
But to himself so secret and so close,
So far from sounding and discovery,
As is the bud bit with an envious worm,
Ere he can spread his sweet leaves to the air,
Or dedicate his beauty to the sun.
Could we but learn from whence his sorrows grow,
We would as willingly give cure as know.}

Enter Romeo

Benvolio. See, where he comes: so please you step aside,
I'll know his grievance, or be much denied.
Montague. I would thou wert so happy by thy stay,
To hear true shrift. Come, madam, let's away.
                                    Exeunt Montague and Lady
Benvolio. Good morrow, cousin.
Romeo.   Is the day so young?

Benvolio. But new struck nine.

Romeo.   Ay me! sad hours seem long.
  Was that my father that went hence so fast?

Benvolio. It was. What sorrow lengthens Romeo's hours?

Romeo. Not having that which, having, makes them short.

Benvolio. In love?

Romeo. Out—

Benvolio. Of love?

Romeo. Out of her favour, where I am in love.

Benvolio. Alas, that love, so gentle in his view,
  Should be so tyrannous and rough in proof!

Romeo. Alas, that love, whose view is muffled still.
  Should without eyes see pathways to his will!
  Where shall we dine? God's me, what fray was here?
  Yet tell me not, for I have heard it all.
  Here's much to do with hate, but more with love:
  Why, then, O brawling love! O loving hate!
  O any thing, of nothing first create!
  O heavy lightness! serious vanity!
  Mis-shapen chaos of well-seeming forms!
  Feather of lead, bright smoke, cold fire, sick health!
  Still-waking sleep, that is not what it is!
  This love feel I, that feel no love in this.
  Dost thou not laugh?

Benvolio.   No, coz, I rather weep.

Romeo. Good heart, at what?

Benvolio.   At thy good heart's oppression.

Romeo. Why, such is love's transgression.
  Griefs of mine own lie heavy in my breast,
  Which thou wilt propagate, to have it prest
  With more of thine: this love that thou hast shown
  Doth add more grief to too much of mine own.
  Love is a smoke rais'd with the fume of sighs:
  Being purg'd, a fire sparkling in lovers' eyes;
  Being vex'd, a sea raging with lovers' tears:
  What is it else? a madness most discreet,
  A choking gall and a preserving sweet.
  Farewell, my coz.

Benvolio.   Soft! I will go along:

An if you leave me so, you do me wrong.
Romeo. Tut, I have lost myself, I am not here,
   This is not Romeo, he's some other where.
Benvolio. Tell me in sadness, who is that you love?
Romeo. What, shall I groan and tell thee?
Benvolio.   Groan? why, no;
   But sadly tell me who.
Romeo. Bid a sick man in sadness make his will.
   Ah, word ill urg'd to one that is so ill!
   In sadness, cousin, I do love a woman.
Benvolio. I aim'd so right whenas you said you lov'd.
Romeo. A right good mark-man! And she's fair I love.
Benvolio. A right fair mark, fair coz, is soonest hit.
Romeo. Well, in that hit you miss: she'll not be hit
   With Cupid's arrow; she hath Dian's wit,
   And in strong proof of chastity well arm'd,
   From love's weak childish bow she lives unharm'd.
   She will not stay the siege of loving terms,
   {Nor bide the encounter of assailing eyes,}
   Nor ope her lap to saint-seducing gold:
   O, she is rich in beauty, only poor
   That, when she dies, with beauty dies her store.
{*Benvolio.* Then she hath sworn that she will still live
   chaste?
Romeo. She hath, and in that sparing makes huge waste;
   For beauty, starv'd with her severity,
   Cuts beauty off from all posterity.
   She is too fair, too wise, wisely too fair,
   To merit bliss by making me despair:
   She hath forsworn to love; and in that vow
   Do I live dead, that live to tell it now.
Benvolio. Be rul'd by me, forget to think of her.
Romeo. O teach me how I should forget to think.
Benvolio. By giving liberty unto thine eyes.
   Examine other beauties.
Romeo.   'Tis the way
   To call hers, exquisite, in question more:
   These happy masks that kiss fair ladies' brows,
   Being black, put us in mind they hide the fair;

He that is strucken blind cannot forget
The precious treasure of his eyesight lost:
Show me a mistress that is passing fair,
What doth her beauty serve but as a note
Where I may read who pass'd that passing fair?
Farewell: thou canst not teach me to forget.
Benvolio. I'll pay that doctrine, or else die in debt.   *Exeunt*

Scene II

Enter Capulet, Paris, and Servant

Capulet. But Montague is bound as well as I,
    In penalty alike, and 'tis not hard, I think,
    For men so old as we to keep the peace.}
Paris. Of honourable reckoning are you both;
    And pity 'tis you liv'd at odds so long.
    But now, my lord, what say you to my suit?
Capulet. But saying o'er what I have said before:
    My child is yet a stranger in the world,
    She hath not seen the change of fourteen years;
    Let two more summers wither in their pride
    Ere we may think her ripe to be a bride.
Paris. Younger than she are happy mothers made.
Capulet. And too soon marr'd are those so early made.
    {The earth hath swallow'd all my hopes but she,
    She is the hopeful lady of my earth:}
    But woo her, gentle Paris, get her heart;
    My will to her consent is but a part;
    {An she agree, within her scope of choice
    Lies my consent and fair according voice.}
    This night I hold an old accustom'd feast,
    Whereto I have invited many a guest,
    Such as I love; and you among the store,
    One more, most welcome, makes my number more.
    At my poor house look to behold this night
    Earth-treading stars that make dark heaven light:
    Such comfort as do lusty young men feel

When well-apparell'd April on the heel
Of limping winter treads, even such delight
Among fresh female buds shall you this night
Inherit at my house; hear all, all see,
And like her most whose merit most shall be:
Which on more view, of many mine being one
May stand in number, though in reckoning none.
Come, go with me. Go, sirrah, trudge about
Through fair Verona; find those persons out
Whose names are written there, and to them say,
My house and welcome on their pleasure stay.

Exeunt Capulet and Paris

Servant. Find them out whose names are written here! It is
written that the shoemaker should meddle with his
yard and the tailor with his last, the fisher with his
pencil and the painter with his nets; but I am sent to find
those persons whose names are here writ, and can never
find what names the writing person hath here writ. I
must to the learned. In good time.

Enter Benvolio and Romeo

Benvolio. Tut, man, one fire burns out another's burning.
    One pain is lessen'd by another's anguish;
Turn giddy, and be holp by backward turning;
    One desperate grief cures with another's languish:
Take thou some new infection to thy eye,
And the rank poison of the old will die.
Romeo. Your plantain-leaf is excellent for that.
Benvolio. For what, I pray thee?
Romeo.   For your broken shin.
Benvolio. Why, Romeo, art thou mad?
Romeo. Not mad, but bound more than a madman is;
    Shut up in prison, kept without my food,
    Whipt and tormented and— God-den, good fellow.
Servant. God gi' god-den. I pray, sir, can you read?
Romeo. Ay, mine own fortune in my misery.
Servant. Perhaps you have learned it without book: but, I
    pray, can you read anything you see?
Romeo. Ay, if I know the letters and the language.

Servant. Ye say honestly: rest you merry!
Romeo. Stay, fellow; I can read.   *Reads*

> 'Signior Martino and his wife and daughters; County
> Anselme and his beauteous sisters; the lady widow of
> Vitruvio; Signior Placentio and his lovely nieces; Mercu-
> tio and his brother Valentine; mine uncle Capulet, his
> wife, and daughters; my fair niece Rosaline; Livia; Sig-
> nior Valentio and his cousin Tybalt; Lucio and the lively
> Helena.'

A fair assembly: whither should they come?
Servant. Up.
Romeo. Whither? To supper?
Servant. To our house.
Romeo. Whose house?
Servant. My master's.
Romeo. Indeed, I should have ask'd you that before.
Servant. Now I'll tell you without asking: my master is the
    great rich Capulet; and if you be not of the house of
    Montagues, I pray, come and crush a cup of wine.
    Rest you merry!   *Exit*
Benvolio. At this same ancient feast of Capulet's
    Sups the fair Rosaline whom thou so loves,
    With all the admired beauties of Verona:
    Go thither, and with unattainted eye
    Compare her face with some that I shall show,
    And I will make thee think thy swan a crow.
Romeo. When the devout religion of mine eye
        Maintains such falsehood, then turn tears to fires;
    And these, who, often drown'd, could never die,
        Transparent heretics, be burnt for liars!
    One fairer than my love! the all-seeing sun
    Ne'er saw her match since first the world begun.
Benvolio. Tut, you saw her fair, none else being by,
    Herself pois'd with herself in either eye:
    But in that crystal scales let there be weigh'd
    Your lady's love against some other maid,
    That I will show you shining at this feast,

And she shall scant show well that now seems best.
Romeo. I'll go along, no such sight to be shown,
But to rejoice in splendour of mine own.   *Exeunt*

Scene III

A room in Capulet's house

Enter Lady Capulet and Nurse

Lady Capulet. Nurse, where's my daughter? call her forth
to me.
Nurse. Now, by my maidenhead at twelve year old,
I bade her come. What, lamb! what, lady-bird!—
God forbid!—Where's this girl? What, Juliet!

Enter Juliet

Juliet. How now, who calls?
Nurse. Your mother.
Juliet. Madam, I am here, what is your will?
Lady Capulet. This is the matter. Nurse, give leave awhile,
We must talk in secret:—nurse, come back again;
I have remember'd me, thou's hear our counsel.
Thou know'st my daughter's of a pretty age.
Nurse. Faith, I can tell her age unto an hour.
Lady Capulet. She's not fourteen.
Nurse.   I'll lay fourteen of my teeth,—
And yet, to my teen be it spoken, I have but four,—
She is not fourteen. How long is it now
To Lammas-tide?
Lady Capulet.   A fortnight and odd days.
Nurse. Even or odd, of all days in the year,
Come Lammas-eve at night shall she be fourteen.
Susan and she—God rest all Christian souls!—
Were of an age: well, Susan is with God;
She was too good for me:—but, as I said,
On Lammas-eve at night shall she be fourteen;
That shall she, marry; I remember it well.
'Tis since the earthquake now eleven years;

And she was wean'd,—I never shall forget it—
Of all the days of the year, upon that day:
For I had then laid wormwood to my dug,
Sitting in the sun under the dove-house wall;
My lord and you were then at Mantua:—
Nay, I do bear a brain:—but, as I said,
When it did taste the wormwood on the nipple
Of my dug, and felt it bitter, pretty fool,
To see it tetchy, and fall out with the dug!
Shake, quoth the dove-house: 'twas no need, I trow,
To bid me trudge.
And since that time it is eleven years;
For then she could stand high-lone; nay, by the rood,
She could have run and waddled all about;
For even the day before, she broke her brow:
And then my husband,—God be with his soul!
A' was a merry man—took up the child:
'Yea,' quoth he, 'dost thou fall upon thy face?
Thou wilt fall backward when thou hast more wit;
Wilt thou not, Jule?' and, by my holidame,
The pretty wretch left crying, and said 'Ay.'
To see now how a jest shall come about!
I warrant, an I should live a thousand years,
I never should forget it: 'Wilt thou not, Jule?' quoth he;
And, pretty fool, it stinted, and said 'Ay.'
{*Lady Capulet.* Enough of this; I pray thee, hold thy peace.
Nurse. Yes, madam: yet I cannot choose but laugh,
To think it should leave crying, and say 'Ay':
And yet, I warrant, it had upon its brow
A bump as big as a young cockerel's stone;
A perilous knock; and it cried bitterly:
'Yea,' quoth my husband, 'fall'st upon thy face?
Thou wilt fall backward when thou comest to age;
Wilt thou not, Jule?' it stinted, and said 'Ay.'}
Juliet. And stint thou too, I pray thee, nurse, say I.
Nurse. Peace, I have done. God mark thee to his grace!
Thou wast the prettiest babe that e'er I nurs'd:
An I might live to see thee married once,

I have my wish.
Lady Capulet. Marry, that 'marry' is the very theme
    I came to talk of. Tell me, daughter Juliet,
    How stands your disposition to be married?
Juliet. It is an honour that I dream not of.
Nurse. An honour! were not I thine only nurse,
    I would say thou hadst suck'd wisdom from thy teat.
Lady Capulet. {Well, think of marriage now; younger than you
    Here in Verona, ladies of esteem,
    Are made already mothers. By my count,
    I was your mother much upon these years
    That you are now a maid. Thus then in brief;}
    The valiant Paris seeks you for his love.
Nurse. A man, young lady! lady, such a man
    As all the world—why, he's a man of wax.
Lady Capulet. Verona's summer hath not such a flower.
Nurse. Nay, he's a flower; in faith, a very flower.
{*Lady Capulet.* What say you? can you love the gentleman?
    This night you shall behold him at our feast:
    Read o'er the volume of young Paris' face,
    And find delight writ there with beauty's pen;
    Examine every married lineament,
    And see how one another lends content;
    And what obscur'd in this fair volume lies
    Find written in the margent of his eyes.
    This precious book of love, this unbound lover,
    To beautify him, only lacks a cover:
    The fish lives in the sea; and 'tis much pride
    For fair without the fair within to hide:
    That book in many's eyes doth share the glory,
    That in gold clasps locks in the golden story:
    So shall you share all that he doth possess,
    By having him making yourself no less.
Nurse. No less! nay, bigger: women grow by men.}
Lady Capulet. Speak briefly, can you like of Paris' love?
Juliet. I'll look to like, if looking liking move:
    But no more deep will I endart mine eye

Than your consent gives strength to make it fly.

Enter a Servingman

Servingman. Madam, the guests are come, supper served up, you called, my young lady asked for, the nurse cursed in the pantry, and every thing in extremity. I must hence to wait; I beseech you, follow straight.

{*Lady Capulet.* We follow thee. (*exit Servingman.*) Juliet, the county stays.

Nurse. Go, girl, seek happy nights to happy days.}   *Exeunt*

Scene IV

A *street*

Enter Romeo, Mercutio, Benvolio, with five or six other Maskers, and Torch-bearers

Romeo. What, shall this speech be spoke for our excuse?
  Or shall we on without apology?
Benvolio. The date is out of such prolixity:
  We'll have no Cupid hoodwink'd with a scarf,
  Bearing a Tartar's painted bow of lath,
  Scaring the ladies like a crow-keeper;
  [Nor no without-book prologue, faintly spoke
  After the prompter, for our entrance:]
  But, let them measure us by what they will,
  We'll measure them a measure, and be gone.
Romeo. Give me a torch: I am not for this ambling;
  Being but heavy, I will bear the light.
Mercutio. Nay, gentle Romeo, we must have you dance.
Romeo. Not I, believe me: you have dancing shoes
  With nimble soles: I have a soul of lead
  So stakes me to the ground, I cannot stir.
{*Mercutio.* You are a lover, borrow Cupid's wings,
  And soar with them above a common bound.
Romeo. I am too sore enpierced with his shaft
  To soar with his light feathers, and so bound,
  I cannot bound a pitch above dull woe:

Under love's heavy burthen do I sink.
Mercutio. And, to sink in it, should you burthen love;
  Too great oppression for a tender thing.
Romeo. Is love a tender thing? it is too rough,
  Too rude, too boisterous, and it pricks like thorn.
Mercutio. If love be rough with you, be rough with love,
  Prick love for pricking, and you beat love down.}
  Give me a case to put my visage in:
  A visor for a visor! what care I
  What curious eye doth cote deformities?
  {Here are the beetle-brows shall blush for me.
Benvolio. Come, knock and enter, and no sooner in
  But every man betake him to his legs.}
Romeo. A torch for me, let wantons light of heart
  Tickle the senseless rushes with their heels;
  For I am proverb'd with a grandsire phrase;
  I'll be a candle-holder, and look on.
  The game was ne'er so fair, and I am done.
Mercutio. Tut, dun's the mouse, the constable's old word:
  If thou art dun, we'll draw thee from the mire
  Of this sir-reverence love, wherein thou stick'st
  Up to the ears. Come, we burn daylight, ho.
Romeo. Nay, that's not so.
Mercutio.   I mean, sir, in delay
  We waste our lights in vain, like lamps by day.
  Take our good meaning, for our judgement sits
  Five times in that ere once in our five wits.
Romeo. And we mean well, in going to this mask;
  But 'tis no wit to go.
Mercutio.   Why, may one ask?
Romeo. I dreamt a dream to-night.
Mercutio.   And so did I.
Romeo. Well, what was yours?
Mercutio.   That dreamers often lie.
Romeo. In bed asleep, while they do dream things true.
Mercutio. Ah, then, I see Queen Mab hath been with you.
[*Benvolio.* Queen Mab? What's she?
Mercutio.] She is the fairies' midwife, and she comes

In shape no bigger than an agate-stone
On the fore-finger of a burgomaster,
Drawn with a team of little atomies
Athwart men's noses when they lie asleep:
Her waggon-spokes are made of spinners' webs;
The cover, of the wings of grasshoppers;
The traces are the moonshine's watery beams;
The collars cricket's bones; the lash, of films;
Her waggoner is a small grey-coated fly,
Not half so big as is a little worm
Prick'd from the lazy finger of a maid:
{Her chariot is an empty hazel-nut,
Made by the joiner squirrel or old grub,
Time out o' mind the fairies' coachmakers.}
And in this state she gallops night by night
Through lovers' brains, and then they dream of love;
O'er courtiers' knees, that dream on court'sies straight;
{O'er lawyers' fingers, who straight dream on fees;}
O'er ladies' lips, who straight on kisses dream,
Which oft the angry Mab with blisters plagues,
Because their breaths with sweetmeats tainted are:
Sometime she gallops o'er a lawyer's lap,
And then dreams he of smelling out a suit;
And sometime comes she with a tithe-pig's tail
Tickling a parson's nose that lies asleep,
Then dreams he of another benefice:
Sometime she driveth o'er a soldier's neck,
And then dreams he of cutting foreign throats,
Of breaches, ambuscadoes, counter-mines,
Of healths five fathom deep; and then anon
Drums in his ear, at which he starts and wakes,
And {being thus frighted} swears a prayer or two,
And sleeps again. This is that very Mab
That plaits the manes of horses in the night,
And bakes the elf-locks in foul sluttish hairs,
Which once untangled much misfortune breeds:
This is the hag, when maids lie on their backs,
{That presses them and learns them first to bear,}

Making them women of good carriage:
{This is she—}
Romeo.   Peace, peace, Mercutio, peace!
Thou talk'st of nothing.
Mercutio.   True, I talk of dreams;
Which are the children of an idle brain,
Begot of nothing but vain fantasy,
Which is as thin of substance as the air,
And more inconstant than the wind, who woos
Even now the frozen bosom of the north,
And, being anger'd, puffs away in haste,
Turning his face to the dew-dropping south.
Benvolio. This wind you talk of blows us from ourselves;
Supper is done, and we shall come too late.
Romeo. I fear, too early, for my mind misgives,
Some consequence yet hanging in the stars,
Shall bitterly begin his fearful date
With this night's revels, and expire the term
Of a despised life clos'd in my breast,
By some untimely forfeit of vile death:
But He, that hath the steerage of my course,
Direct my sail! On, lusty gentlemen.
{*Benvolio.* Strike, drum.}
                              {*They march about the stage, and Servingmen
                                come forth with napkins*

Scene V

First Serv. Where's Potpan, that he helps not to take away?
he shift a trencher, he scrape a trencher?
Sec. Serv. When good manners shall lie all in one or two
men's hands, and they unwash'd too, 'tis a foul thing.
First Serv. Away with the joint-stools, remove the court-
cupboard, look to the plate. Good thou, save me a piece
of marchpane; and, as thou loves me, let the porter let in
Susan Grindstone and Nell. Antony and Potpan!

Sec. Serv. Ay, boy, ready.

First Serv. You are look'd for and call'd for, ask'd for and
sought for, in the great chamber.

Third Serv. We cannot be here and there too. Cheerly,
boys; be brisk a while, and the longer liver take all.

They retire behind}

Enter Capulet, Juliet, and Guests to the Maskers

Capulet. Welcome, gentlemen! ladies that have their toes
Unplagu'd with corns will have a bout with you:
Ah ha, my mistresses! which of you all
Will now deny to dance? She that makes dainty,
She, I'll swear, hath corns; am I come near ye now?
Welcome, gentlemen! {I have seen the day
That I have worn a visor, and could tell
A whispering tale in a fair lady's ear,
Such as would please: 'tis gone, 'tis gone, 'tis gone:
You are welcome, gentlemen! Come, musicians, play.
A hall, a hall! give room! and foot it, girls.

Music plays, and they dance}

More lights, you knaves; and turn the tables up,
And quench the fire, the room is grown too hot.
Ah, sirrah, this unlook'd-for sport comes well.
Nay, sit, nay, sit, good cousin Capulet;
For you and I are past our standing days:
How long is 't now since last yourself and I
Were in a mask?

Sec. Capulet. By 'r lady, thirty years.

Capulet. What, man! 'tis not so much, 'tis not so much:
'Tis since the nuptial of Lucentio,
Come Pentecost as quickly as it will,
Some five and twenty years; and then we mask'd.

Sec. Capulet. 'Tis more, 'tis more: his son is elder, sir;
{His son is thirty.}

Capulet.   Will you tell me that?
His son was but a ward two years ago.
[Good youths, i' faith: oh youth's a jolly thing!]

Romeo. (to a Servingman) What lady's that, which doth enrich the hand
    Of yonder knight?
{*Servingman.* I know not, sir.}
Romeo. O, she doth teach the torches to burn bright!
    It seems she hangs upon the cheek of night
    Like a rich jewel in an Ethiop's ear;
    Beauty too rich for use, for earth too dear!
    So shines a snow-white swan trooping with crows,
    As this fair lady o'er her fellows shows.
    The measure done, I'll watch her place of stand,
    And, touching hers, make blessed my rude hand.
    Did my heart love till now? forswear it, sight!
    I never saw true beauty till this night.
Tybalt. This, by his voice, should be a Montague.
    Fetch me my rapier, boy. What dares the slave
    Come hither, cover'd with an antic face,
    To fleer and scorn at our solemnity?
    Now, by the stock and honour of my kin,
    To strike him dead I hold it not a sin.
Capulet. Why, how now, kinsman! wherefore storm you so?
Tybalt. Uncle, this is a Montague, our foe;
    A villain, that is hither come in spite,
    To scorn at our solemnity this night.
Capulet. Young Romeo is it?
Tybalt.   'Tis he, that villain Romeo.
Capulet. Content thee, gentle coz, let him alone,
    He bears him like a portly gentleman;
    And, to say truth, Verona brags of him
    To be a virtuous and well-govern'd youth:
    I would not for the wealth of all this town
    Here in my house do him disparagement:
    Therefore be patient, take no note of him:
    {It is my will, the which if thou respect,}
    Show a fair presence and put off these frowns,
    An ill-beseeming semblance for a feast.
Tybalt. It fits, when such a villain is a guest:
    I'll not endure him.
Capulet.   He shall be endur'd:

What, goodman boy! I say, he shall: go to;
Am I the master here, or you? go to.
You'll not endure him? God shall mend my soul,
You'll make a mutiny among my guests:
You will set cock-a-hoop, you'll be the man!
Tybalt. Why, uncle, 'tis a shame.
Capulet.   Go to, go to;
You are a saucy boy, is 't so, indeed?
This trick may chance to scathe you, I know what:
{You must contrary me! marry, 'tis time.}
Well said, my hearts! {You are a princox; go:}
Be quiet, or— More light, more light! For shame!
I'll make you quiet. What, cheerly, my hearts!
Tybalt. Patience perforce with wilful choler meeting
Makes my flesh tremble in their different greeting.
I will withdraw, but this intrusion shall,
Now seeming sweet, convert to bitter gall.   *Exit*
Romeo. (*to Juliet*) If I profane with my unworthiest hand
This holy shrine, the gentle sin is this,
My lips, two blushing pilgrims, ready stand
To smooth the rough touch with a gentle kiss.
Juliet. Good pilgrim, you do wrong your hand too much,
Which mannerly devotion shows in this;
For saints have hands that pilgrims' hands do touch,
And palm to palm is holy palmers' kiss.
Romeo. Have not saints lips, and holy palmers too?
Juliet. Ay, pilgrim, lips that they must use in prayer.
Romeo. O, then, fair saint, let lips do what hands do;
They pray, grant thou, lest faith turn to despair.
Juliet. Saints do not move, though grant for prayers' sake.
Romeo. Then move not, while my prayer's effect I take.
Thus from my lips by thine my sin is purg'd.

                                        Kissing her

Juliet. Then have my lips the sin that they have took.
Romeo. Sin from my lips? O trespass sweetly urg'd!
Give me my sin again.
Juliet.   You kiss by the book.
Nurse. Madam, your mother craves a word with you.
Romeo. What is her mother?

Nurse.   Marry, bachelor,
   Her mother is the lady of the house,
   And a good lady, and a wise and virtuous:
   I nurs'd her daughter, that you talk'd withal;
   I tell you, he that can lay hold of her
   Shall have the chinks.
Romeo.   Is she a Capulet?
   O dear account! my life is my foe's thrall.
{*Benvolio.* Away, be gone, the sport is at the best.
Romeo. Ay, so I fear; the more is my unrest.}
Capulet. Nay, gentlemen, prepare not to be gone;
   We have a trifling foolish banquet towards.
                        They whisper in his ear
   Is it e'en so? why, then, I thank you all;
   I thank you, honest gentlemen, good night.
   More torches here! Come on then, let's to bed.
   Ah, sirrah, by my fay, it waxes late:
   I'll to my rest.   *Exeunt all but Juliet and Nurse*
Juliet. Come hither, nurse. What is yond gentleman?
Nurse. The son and heir of old Tiberio.
Juliet. What's he that now is going out of door?
Nurse. Marry, that, I think, be young Petruchio.
Juliet. What's he that follows there, that would not dance?
Nurse. I know not.
Juliet. Go ask his name. If he be married,
   My grave is like to be my wedding bed.
Nurse. His name is Romeo, and a Montague,
   The only son of your great enemy.
Juliet. My only love sprung from my only hate!
   Too early seen unknown, and known too late!
   Prodigious birth of love it is to me,
   That I must love a loathed enemy.
Nurse. What's this? what's this?
Juliet.   A rhyme I learn'd even now
   Of one I danc'd with.   *One calls within* 'Juliet'
Nurse.   Anon, anon!
   Come, let's away; the strangers all are gone.   *Exeunt*

ACT II

{Enter Chorus

Chorus. Now old desire doth in his death-bed lie,
  And young affection gapes to be his heir;
That fair for which love groan'd for and would die,
  With tender Juliet match'd, is now not fair.
Now Romeo is belov'd and loves again,
  Alike bewitched by the charm of looks,
But to his foe suppos'd he must complain,
  And she steal love's sweet bait from fearful hooks:
Being held a foe, he may not have access
  To breathe such vows as lovers used to swear;
And she as much in love, her means much less
  To meet her new beloved any where:
But passion lends them power, time means to meet,
Tempering extremities with extreme sweet.   *Exit}*

Scene I

Enter Romeo, alone

Romeo. Can I go forward when my heart is here?
    Turn back, dull earth, and find thy centre out.
          He climbs the wall, and leaps down within it

Enter Benvolio with Mercutio

Benvolio. Romeo! my cousin Romeo!
Mercutio.   He is wise;
    And, on my life, hath stol'n him home to bed.
Benvolio. He ran this way, and leap'd this orchard wall:
    Call, good Mercutio.
Mercutio.   Call? nay, I'll conjure too.
    Romeo! humours! madman! passion! lover!
    Appear thou in the likeness of a sigh:
    Speak but one rhyme, and I am satisfied;
    Cry but 'ay me!' pronounce but 'love' and 'dove;'
    Speak to my gossip Venus one fair word,
    One nick-name for her purblind son and heir,
    Young Adam Cupid, he that shot so trim
    When King Cophetua lov'd the beggar-wench!
    He heareth not, {he stirreth not, he moveth not;
    The ape is dead, and I must conjure him.}
    I conjure thee by Rosaline's bright eyes,
    By her high forehead and her scarlet lip,
    By her fine foot, straight leg, and quivering thigh,
    And the demesnes that there adjacent lie,
    That in thy likeness thou appear to us!
Benvolio. An if he hear thee, thou wilt anger him.
Mercutio. This cannot anger him: 'twould anger him
    To raise a spirit in his mistress' circle
    Of some strange fashion, making it there to stand
    Till she had laid it and conjur'd it down;
    That were some spite: my invocation
    Is fair and honest, in his mistress' name

I conjure only but to raise up him.
Benvolio. Come, he hath hid himself among these trees,
To be consorted with the humorous night:
Blind is his love, and best befits the dark.
Mercutio. If love be blind, love cannot hit the mark.
Now will he sit under a medlar-tree,
And wish his mistress were that kind of fruit
As maids call medlars when they laugh alone.
O, Romeo, that she were, O, that she were
An open et cetera, thou a poperin pear!
Romeo, good night: I'll to my truckle-bed;
This field-bed is too cold for me to sleep:
Come, shall we go?
Benvolio. Go then, for 'tis but vain
To seek him here that means not to be found. *Exeunt*

Scene II

Capulet's orchard

Enter Romeo

Romeo. He jests at scars that never felt a wound.
Juliet appears above at a window
But, soft! what light through yonder window breaks?
It is the east, and Juliet is the sun!
Arise, fair sun, and kill the envious moon,
Who is already sick and pale with grief,
That thou her maid art far more fair than she:
Be not her maid, since she is envious;
Her vestal livery is but sick and green,
And none but fools do wear it; cast it off.
{It is my lady; O, it is my love!
O, that she knew she were!}
She speaks, yet she says nothing: what of that?
Her eye discourses, I will answer it.
I am too bold, 'tis not to me she speaks:
Two of the fairest stars in all the heaven,
Having some business, do intreat her eyes

To twinkle in their spheres till they return.
What if her eyes were there, they in her head?
The brightness of her cheek would shame those stars,
As daylight doth a lamp; her eyes in heaven
Would through the airy region stream so bright
That birds would sing and think it were not night.
See, how she leans her cheek upon her hand!
I would I were the glove to that same hand,
That I might touch that cheek!

Juliet.   Ay me:
Romeo.   She speaks
    O, speak again, bright angel! for thou art
    As glorious to this night, being o'er my head,
    As is a winged messenger of heaven
    Unto the white-upturned wondering eyes
    Of mortals that fall back to gaze on him,
    When he bestrides the lazy-pacing clouds
    And sails upon the bosom of the air.

Juliet. O Romeo, Romeo! wherefore art thou Romeo?
    Deny thy father and refuse thy name;
    Or, if thou wilt not, be but sworn my love,
    And I'll no longer be a Capulet.

Romeo. (*aside*) Shall I hear more, or shall I speak at this?

Juliet. 'Tis but thy name that is my enemy;
    {Thou art thyself, though not a Montague.}
    What's Montague? it is nor hand, nor foot,
    Nor arm, nor face, nor any other part
    {Belonging to a man. O, be some other name!}
    What's in a name? that which we call a rose
    By any other name would smell as sweet;
    So Romeo would, were he not Romeo call'd,
    Retain that dear perfection which he owes
    Without that title. Romeo, doff thy name,
    And for that name, which is no part of thee,
    Take all I have.

Romeo.   I take thee at thy word:
    Call me but love, and I'll be new baptiz'd;
    Henceforth I never will be Romeo.

Juliet. What man art thou, that, thus bescreen'd in night,
    So stumblest on my counsel?
Romeo.   By a name
    I know not how to tell thee who I am:
    My name, dear saint, is hateful to myself,
    Because it is an enemy to thee;
    Had I it written, I would tear the word.
Juliet. My ears have not yet drunk a hundred words
    Of thy tongue's utterance, yet I know the sound:
    Art thou not Romeo, and a Montague?
Romeo. Neither, fair maid, if either thee dislike.
Juliet. How camest thou hither, tell me, and wherefore?
    The orchard walls are high and hard to climb,
    And the place death, considering who thou art,
    If any of my kinsmen find thee here.
Romeo. With love's light wings did I o'er-perch these walls,
    For stony limits cannot hold love out:
    And what love can do, that dares love attempt;
    Therefore thy kinsmen are no let to me.
Juliet. If they do find thee, they will murder thee.
Romeo. Alack, there lies more peril in thine eye
    Than twenty of their swords: look thou but sweet,
    And I am proof against their enmity.
Juliet. I would not for the world they should find thee here.
Romeo. I have night's cloak to hide me from their eyes;
    And but thou love me, let them find me here:
    For life were better ended by their hate,
    Than death prorogued, wanting of thy love.
Juliet. By whose directions found'st thou out this place?
Romeo. By love, that first did prompt me to inquire;
    He lent me counsel, and I lent him eyes.
    I am no pilot; yet, wert thou as far
    As that vast shore wash'd with the farthest sea,
    I would adventure for such merchandise.
Juliet. Thou know'st the mask of night is on my face,
    Else would a maiden blush bepaint my cheeks
    For that which thou hast heard me speak to-night.
    Fain would I dwell on form, fain, fain, deny
    What I have spoke, but farewell compliments!

Dost thou love me? I know thou wilt say 'Ay,'
And I will take thy word: yet, if thou swear'st,
Thou mayst prove false: at lovers' perjuries,
They say, Jove smiles. O gentle Romeo,
If thou dost love, pronounce it faithfully:
Or if thou think'st I am too easily won,
I'll frown and be perverse, and say thee nay,
So thou wilt woo, but else, not for the world.
In truth, fair Montague, I am too fond;
And therefore thou mayst think my 'haviour light:
But trust me, gentleman, I'll prove more true
Than those that have more cunning to be strange.
I should have been more strange, I must confess,
But that thou overheard'st, ere I was ware,
My true love's passion: therefore pardon me,
And not impute this yielding to light love,
Which the dark night hath so discovered.

Romeo. Lady, by yonder blessed moon I swear,
   That tips with silver all these fruit-tree tops,—

Juliet. O, swear not by the moon, th' inconstant moon,
   That monthly changeth in her circled orb,
   Lest that thy love prove likewise variable.

Romeo. What shall I swear by?

Juliet.   Do not swear at all:
   Or, if thou wilt, swear by thy gracious self,
   Which art the god of my idolatry,
   And I'll believe thee.

Romeo.   If my true heart's love—

Juliet. Well, do not swear: although I joy in thee,
   I have small joy of this contract to-night:
   It is too rash, too unadvis'd, too sudden,
   Too like the lightning, which doth cease to be
   Ere one can say 'It lightens.' {Sweet, good night!
   This bud of love, by summer's ripening breath,
   May prove a beauteous flower when next we meet.
   Good night, good night! as sweet repose and rest
   Come to thy heart as that within my breast!

Romeo. O, wilt thou leave me so unsatisfied?

Juliet. What satisfaction canst thou have to-night:

Romeo. The exchange of thy love's faithful vow for mine.
Juliet. I gave thee mine before thou didst request it:
   And yet I would it were to give again.
Romeo. Wouldst thou withdraw it? for what purpose, love?
Juliet. But to be frank, and give it thee again.
   And yet I wish but for the thing I have:
   My bounty is as boundless as the sea,
   My love as deep; the more I give to thee,
   The more I have, for both are infinite.}
   I hear some noise within; dear love, adieu!

Nurse calls within

   Anon, good nurse! Sweet Montague, be true.
   Stay but a little, I will come again.   *Exit*
Romeo. O blessed, blessed night! I am afeard,
   Being in night, all this is but a dream,
   Too flattering-sweet to be substantial.

Re-enter Juliet, above

Juliet. Three words, dear Romeo, and good night indeed.
   If that thy bent of love be honourable,
   Thy purpose marriage, send me word to-morrow,
   By one that I'll procure to come to thee,
   Where and what time thou wilt perform the rite,
   And all my fortunes at thy foot I'll lay,
   And follow thee my lord throughout the world.
{*Nurse.* (*within*) Madam!
Juliet. I come, anon.—But if thou mean'st not well,
   I do beseech thee—
Nurse. (*within*) Madam!
Juliet.   By and by, I come:—
   To cease thy suit, and leave me to my grief:
   To-morrow will I send.
Romeo.   So thrive my soul,—
Juliet. A thousand times good night!   *Exit*
Romeo. A thousand times the worse, to want thy light.}
   Love goes toward love, as schoolboys from their books,
   But love from love, toward school with heavy looks.

Retiring slowly

Re-enter Juliet

Juliet. Hist! Romeo, hist!—O, for a falconer's voice,
  To lure this tassel-gentle back again!
  Bondage is hoarse, and may not speak aloud;
  Else would I tear the cave where Echo lies,
  And make her airy tongue more hoarse than mine,
  With repetition of my Romeo's name.
  Romeo!
Romeo. It is my soul that calls upon my name:
  How silver-sweet sound lovers' tongues in night,
  {Like softest music to attending ears!}
Juliet. Romeo!
Romeo.   Madame?
Juliet.   At what o'clock to-morrow
  Shall I send to thee?
Romeo.   At the hour of nine.
Juliet. I will not fail: 'tis twenty years till then.
  I have forgot why I did call thee back.
Romeo. Let me stay here till thou remember it.
Juliet. I shall forget, to have thee still stay there,
  Remembering how I love thy company.
Romeo. And I'll still stay, to have thee still forget,
  Forgetting any other home but this.
Juliet. 'Tis almost morning; I would have thee gone:
  And yet no farther than a wanton's bird,
  Who lets it hop a little from her hand,
  Like a poor prisoner in his twisted gyves,
  And with a silk thread plucks it back again,
  So loving-jealous of his liberty.
Romeo. I would I were thy bird.
Juliet.   Sweet, so would I:
  Yet I should kill thee with much cherishing thee.
  Good night, good night! parting is such sweet sorrow
  That I shall say good night till it be morrow.   *Exit*
Romeo. Sleep dwell upon thine eyes, peace on thy breast!
  Would I were sleep and peace, so sweet to rest!
  Now will I to my ghostly father's cell,
  His help to crave, and my good hap to tell.   *Exit*

Scene III

Enter Friar Laurence, with a basket

Friar Laurence. The grey-eyed morn smiles on the frowning
    night,
  Chequering the eastern clouds with streaks of light;
  And flecked darkness like a drunkard reels
  From forth day's path and Titan's fiery wheels:
  Now, ere the sun advance his burning eye,
  The world to cheer and night's dank dew to dry,
  I must up-fill this osier cage of ours
  With baleful weeds and precious-juiced flowers.
  {The earth that's nature's mother is her tomb;
  What is her burying grave, that is her womb:
  And from her womb children of divers kind
  We sucking on her natural bosom find,
  Many for many virtues excellent,
  None but for some, and yet all different.}
  O, mickle is the powerful grace that lies
  In herbs, plants, stones, and their true qualities:
  For nought so vile that on the earth doth live,
  But to the earth some special good doth give;
  Nor aught so good, but, strain'd from that fair use,
  Revolts from true birth, stumbling on abuse:
  Virtue itself turns vice, being misapplied,
  And vice sometime 's by action dignified.
  Within the infant rind of this weak flower
  Poison hath residence, and medicine power:
  For this, being smelt, with that part cheers each part,
  Being tasted, slays all senses with the heart.
  Two such opposed foes encamp them still
  In man as well as herbs, grace and rude will;
  And where the worser is predominant,
  Full soon the canker death eats up that plant.

Enter Romeo

Romeo. Good morrow, father.

Friar Laurence.   Benedicite!
What early tongue so soon saluteth me?
Young son, it argues a distemper'd head
So soon to bid good morrow to thy bed:
Care keep his watch in every old man's eye,
And where care lodges, sleep can never lie;
But where unbruised youth with unstuff'd brain
Doth couch his limbs, there golden sleep doth reign:
Therefore thy earliness doth me assure
Thou art up-rous'd by some distemperature;
Or if not so, then here I hit it right,
Our Romeo hath not been in bed to-night.

Romeo. That last is true; the sweeter rest was mine.

Friar Laurence. God pardon sin! wast thou with Rosaline?

Romeo. With Rosaline, my ghostly father? no;
I have forgot that name and that name's woe.

Friar Laurence. That's my good son: but where hast thou
    been then?

Romeo. I'll tell thee ere thou ask it me again.
I have been feasting with mine enemy,
Where on a sudden one hath wounded me,
That's by me wounded: both our remedies
Within thy help and holy physic lies:
I bear no hatred, blessed man, for, lo,
My intercession likewise steads my foe.

Friar Laurence. Be plain, good son, and homely in thy drift;
Riddling confession finds but riddling shrift.

Romeo. Then plainly know my heart's dear love is set
On the fair daughter of rich Capulet:
As mine on hers, so hers likewise on mine;
And all combin'd, save what thou must combine
By holy marriage: where, and when, and how,
We met, we woo'd and made exchange of vow,
I'll tell thee as we pass; but this I pray,
That thou consent to marry us to-day.

Friar Laurence. Holy Saint Francis, what a change is here!
Is Rosaline, that thou didst love so dear,
So soon forsook? lo! young men's love then lies

Not truly in their hearts, but in their eyes.
Jesu Maria, what a deal of brine
Hath wash'd thy sallow cheeks for Rosaline!
How much salt water cast away in waste,
To season love, that of love doth not taste!
The sun not yet thy sighs from heaven clears,
Thy old groans ring yet in mine ancient ears;
Lo, here upon thy cheek the stain doth sit
Of an old tear that is not wash'd off yet:
If e'er thou wast thyself, and these woes thine,
Thou and these woes were all for Rosaline:
And art thou chang'd? pronounce this sentence then:
Women may fall, when there's no strength in men.
Romeo. Thou chidd'st me oft for loving Rosaline.
Friar Laurence. For doting, not for loving, pupil mine.
Romeo. And bad'st me bury love.
Friar Laurence.   Not in a grave,
    To lay one in, another out to have.
Romeo. I pray thee, chide not: she whom I love now
    Doth grace for grace and love for love allow;
    The other did not so.
Friar Laurence.   O, she knew well
    Thy love did read by rote, and could not spell.
    But come, young waverer, come, go with me,
    In one respect I'll thy assistant be;
    For this alliance may so happy prove,
    To turn your households' rancour to pure love.
{*Romeo.* O, let us hence; I stand on sudden haste.
Friar Laurence. Wisely and slow; they stumble that run
        fast.}   *Exeunt*

Scene IV

A street

Enter Benvolio and Mercutio

Mercutio. Where the devil should this Romeo be?
  Came he not home to-night?
Benvolio. Not to his father's, I spoke with his man.
Mercutio. Ah, that same pale hard-hearted wench, that
    Rosaline,
  Torments him so that he will sure run mad.
Benvolio. Tybalt, the kinsman to old Capulet,
  Hath sent a letter to his father's house.
Mercutio. A challenge, on my life.
Benvolio. Romeo will answer it.
Mercutio. Any man that can write may answer a letter.
Benvolio. Nay, he will answer the letter's master, how he
  dares, being dar'd.
Mercutio. Alas, poor Romeo, he is already dead! stabbed
  with a white wench's black eye, shot thorough the ear
  with a love-song, the very pin of his heart cleft with the
  blind bow-boy's butt-shaft, and is he a man to encounter
  Tybalt?
Benvolio. Why, what is Tybalt?
Mercutio. More than the prince of cats, [I can tell you.] O,
  he's the courageous captain of compliments. [Catso!] He
  fights as you sing prick-song, keeps time, distance and
  proportion; rests me his minim rest, one, two, and the
  third in your bosom: the very butcher of a silk button, a
  duellist, a duellist; a gentleman of the very first house, of
  the first and second cause: ah, the immortal passado! the
  punto reverso! the hai!
Benvolio. The what?
Mercutio. The pox of such antic, lisping, affecting fantasti-
  coes; these new tuners of accents! 'By Jesu, a very good
  blade! a very tall man! a very good whore!' Why, is not
  this a miserable case, grandsire, that we should be still af-
  flicted with these strange flies, these fashion-mongers,

these pardon-mes, who stand so much on the new form
that they cannot sit at ease on the old bench? O, their
bones, their bones!

Enter Romeo

Benvolio. Here comes Romeo, here comes Romeo.

Mercutio. Without his roe, like a dried herring: O flesh,
flesh, how art thou fishified! Now is he for the numbers
that Petrarch flowed in: Laura to his lady was but a
kitchen-drudge; yet she had a better love to berhyme her;
Dido, a dowdy, Cleopatra, a gipsy, Helen and Hero, hil-
dings and harlotries; Thisbe, a grey eye or so, but not to
the purpose. Signior Romeo, bon jour! there's a French
courtesy to your French slop. You gave us the counterfeit
fairly last night.

Romeo. Good morrow to you both. What counterfeit did I
give you?

Mercutio. The slip, the slip; can you not conceive?

Romeo. Pardon, good Mercutio, my business was great, and
in such a case as mine a man may strain courtesy.

Mercutio. That's as much as to say, Such a case as yours
constrains a man to bow in the hams.

{*Romeo.* Meaning, to court'sy.

Mercutio. Thou hast most kindly hit it.}

Romeo. A most courteous exposition.

Mercutio. Nay, I am the very pink of courtesy.

Romeo. Pink for flower?

Mercutio. Right.

Romeo. Why, then is my pump well flower'd.

Mercutio. Well said: follow me this jest now, till thou hast
worn out thy pump, that, when the single sole of it is
worn, the jest may remain, after the wearing, solely singular.

Romeo. O single-sol'd jest, solely singular for the singleness!

Mercutio. Come between us, good Benvolio; my wits fail.

Romeo. Switch and spurs, switch and spurs, or I'll cry a
match.

Mercutio. Nay, if thy wits run the wild-goose chase, I have done; for thou hast more of the wild-goose in one of thy wits than, {I am sure,} I have in all my five: was I with you there for the goose?

Romeo. Thou wast never with me for anything when thou wast not with me for the goose.

Mercutio. I will bite thee by the ear for that jest.

Romeo. Nay, good goose, bite not.

Mercutio. Thy wit is a very bitter sweeting, a most sharp sauce.

Romeo. And is it not well serv'd in to a sweet goose?

Mercutio. O, here's a wit of cheveril, that stretches from an inch narrow to an ell broad!

Romeo. I stretch it out for that word 'broad;' which added to the goose, proves thee far and wide a broad goose.

Mercutio. Why, is not this better now than groaning for love? now art thou sociable, now art thou thyself; now art thou what thou art, as well by art as nature: for this drivelling love is like a great natural, that runs {lolling} up and down to hide his bauble in a hole.

Benvolio. Stop there, {stop there.}

Mercutio. Why, thou wouldst have me stop my tale against the hair?

Benvolio. Thou wouldst else have made thy tale too long.

Mercutio. Tut, man, thou art deceiv'd; I would have made it short: for I was come to the whole depth of my tale, and meant indeed to occupy the argument no longer.

Romeo. Here's goodly gear!

Enter Nurse and Peter

Mercutio. A sail, a sail, a sail!

Benvolio. Two, two; a shirt and a smock.

Nurse. Peter!

Peter. Anon?

Nurse. My fan, Peter.

Mercutio. Good Peter, to hide her face; for her fan's the fairer of the two.

Nurse. God ye good morrow, gentlemen.

Mercutio. God ye good den, fair gentlewoman.

Nurse. Is it good den, I pray you?

Mercutio. 'Tis no less, I assure you, for the bawdy hand of
the dial is now upon the prick of noon.

Nurse. Out upon you, what a man are you!

Romeo. A gentleman, nurse, that God hath made for himself to mar.

Nurse. By my troth, well said; 'for himself to mar,' quoth 'a?
Gentlemen, can any of you tell me where one may find
the young Romeo?

Romeo. I can; but young Romeo will be elder when you
have found him than he was when you sought him: I am
the youngest of that name, for fault of a worse.

Nurse. You say well.

Mercutio. Yea, is the worst well? mass, well noted, wisely,
wisely.

Nurse. If you be he, sir, I desire some conference with you.

Benvolio. She will indite him to some supper.

Mercutio. So ho! A bawd, a bawd, a bawd!

Romeo. Why, what hast found, man?

Mercutio. No hare, sir; unless it be a hare in a lenten pie,
that is something stale and hoar ere it be eaten.

He walks by them and sings

> An old hare hoar,
> And an old hare hoar,
> Is very good meat in lent:
>> But a hare that is hoar,
>> Is too much for a score,
> If it hoar ere it be spent.

Romeo, will you come to your father's? we'll to dinner
thither.

Romeo. I will follow you.

Mercutio. Farewell, ancient lady; farewell, (*singing*) 'lady,
lady, lady.'   *Exeunt Mercutio and Benvolio*

Nurse. [Marry, farewell!] I pray you, sir, what saucy mer-
chant was this, that was so full of his ropery?

Romeo. A gentleman, nurse, that loves to hear himself talk,
and will speak more in a minute than he will stand to in a
month.

Nurse. An a' speak any thing against me, I'll take him down, an a' were lustier than he is, and twenty such Jacks; and if I cannot, I'll find those that shall. Scurvy knave! I am none of his flirt-gills; I am none of his skains-mates. (*turning to Peter*) And thou must stand by too, and suffer every knave to use me at his pleasure?

Peter. I saw no man use you at his pleasure; if I had, my weapon should quickly have been out, I warrant you: I dare draw as soon as another man, if I see occasion in a good quarrel and the law on my side.

Nurse. Now, afore God, I am so vex'd that every part about me quivers. Scurvy knave! Pray you, sir, a word: and as I told you, my young lady bade me inquire you out; what she bade me say, I will keep to myself: but first let me tell ye, if ye should lead her into a fool's paradise, as they say, it were a very gross kind of behaviour, as they say: for the gentlewoman is young, and therefore, if you should deal double with her, truly it were an ill thing to be offered to any gentlewoman, and very weak dealing.

Romeo. Nurse, commend me to thy lady and mistress; tell her I protest—

Nurse. Good heart, and, i' faith, I will tell her as much: Lord, Lord, she will be a joyful woman.

Romeo. What wilt thou tell her, nurse? {thou dost not mark me.}

Nurse. {I will tell her, sir,} that you do protest; which, as I take it, is a gentlemanlike proffer.

Romeo. Bid her devise
Some means to come to shrift this afternoon;
And there she shall at Friar Laurence' cell
Be shriv'd and married. Here is for thy pains.

Nurse. No, truly, sir; not a penny.

Romeo. Go to; I say you shall.

Nurse. This afternoon, sir? well, she shall be there.

Romeo. And stay, good nurse, behind the abbey-wall:
Within this hour my man shall be with thee,
And bring thee cords made like a tackled stair;
Which to the high top-gallant of my joy
Must be my convoy in the secret night.
Farewell; be trusty, and I'll quit thy pains:

Farewell; commend me to thy mistress.
{*Nurse.* Now God in heaven bless thee! Hark you, sir.
Romeo. What say'st thou, my dear nurse?
Nurse. Is your man secret? Did you ne'er hear say,
  Two may keep counsel, putting one away?
Romeo. I warrant thee, my man's as true as steel.
Nurse. Well, sir; my mistress is the sweetest lady—Lord,
  Lord! when 'twas a little prating thing— O, there is a no-
  bleman in town, one Paris, that would fain lay knife
  aboard; but she, good soul, had as lief see a toad, a very
  toad, as see him. I anger her sometimes, and tell her that
  Paris is the properer man; but, I'll warrant you, when I
  say so, she looks as pale as any clout in the versal world.
  Doth not rosemary and Romeo begin both with a letter?
Romeo. Ay, nurse; what of that? both with an R.
Nurse. Ah, mocker! that's the dog's name; R is for the—No;
  I know it begins with some other letter—and she hath the
  prettiest sententious of it, of you and rosemary, that it
  would do you good to hear it.
Romeo. Commend me to thy lady.
Nurse. Ay, a thousand times. (*exit Romeo.*) Peter!
Peter. Anon?}
Nurse. Peter, take my fan and go before, and apace.

                                                    Exeunt

Scene V

Capulet's orchard

Enter Juliet

Juliet. The clock struck nine when I did send my nurse;
  In half an hour she promis'd to return.
  Perchance she cannot find him: that's not so.
  O, she is lame! love's heralds should be thoughts,
  {Which ten times faster glide than the sun's beams,
  Driving back shadows over louring hills:
  Therefore do nimble-pinion'd doves draw love,
  And therefore hath the wind-swift Cupid wings.

Now is the sun upon the highmost hill
Of this day's journey, and from nine till twelve
Is three long hours; yet she is not come.
Had she affections and warm youthful blood,
She would be as swift in motion as a ball;
My words would bandy her to my sweet love,
And his to me:
But old folks, many feign as they were dead;
Unwieldy, slow, heavy, and pale as lead.}

Enter Nurse, with Peter

O God, she comes! O honey nurse, what news?
Hast thou met with him? Send thy man away.
Nurse. Peter, stay at the gate.   *Exit Peter*
Juliet. Now, good sweet nurse,—O Lord, why look'st thou
    sad?
    Though news be sad, yet tell them merrily;
    If good, thou sham'st the music of sweet news
    By playing it to me with so sour a face.
Nurse. I am a-weary, give me leave a while,
    Fie, how my bones ache, what a jaunt have I had!
Juliet. I would thou hadst my bones, and I thy news:
    Nay, come, I pray thee, speak; good, good nurse, speak.
Nurse. Jesu, what haste, can you not stay a while?
    Do you not see that I am out of breath?
Juliet. How art thou out of breath, when thou hast breath
    To say to me that thou art out of breath?
    The excuse that thou dost make in this delay
    Is longer than the tale thou dost excuse.
    Is thy news good, or bad? answer to that;
    Say either, and I'll stay the circumstance:
    Let me be satisfied, is 't good or bad?
Nurse. Well, you have made a simple choice, you know not
    how to choose a man: Romeo! no, not he; though his face
    be better than any man's, yet his leg excels all men's, and
    for a hand, and a foot, and a body, though they be not to
    be talk'd on, yet they are past compare: he is not the
    flower of courtesy, but, I'll warrant him, as gentle as a

lamb. Go thy ways, wench; serve God. What, have you
din'd at home?

Juliet. No, no: but all this did I know before.
What says he of our marriage? what of that?

Nurse. Lord, how my head aches! what a head have I!
It beats as it would fall in twenty pieces.
My back o' t' other side,—ah, my back, my back!
Beshrew your heart for sending me about,
To catch my death with jaunting up and down!

Juliet. I' faith, I am sorry that thou art not well.
Sweet, sweet, sweet nurse, tell me, what says my love?

Nurse. Your love says, like an honest gentleman, and a courteous, and a kind, and a handsome, and, I warrant, a virtuous,—Where is your mother?

Juliet. Where is my mother? why, she is within?
Where should she be? How oddly thou repliest!
'Your love says, like an honest gentleman,
Where is your mother?'

Nurse.   O God's lady dear!
Are you so hot? marry, come up, I trow;
Is this the poultice for my aching bones?
Henceforward do your messages yourself.

Juliet. Here's such a coil! come, what says Romeo?

Nurse. Have you got leave to go to shrift to-day?

Juliet. I have.

Nurse. Then hie you hence to Friar Laurence' cell;
There stays a husband to make you a wife:
Now comes the wanton blood up in your cheeks,
{They'll be in scarlet straight at any news.}
Hie you to church; I must another way,
To fetch a ladder, by the which your love
Must climb a bird's nest soon when it is dark;
I am the drudge, and toil in your delight;
But you shall bear the burthen soon at night.
Go; I'll to dinner; hie you to the cell.

Juliet. Hie to high fortune! Honest nurse, farewell.   *Exeunt*

Scene VI

Friar Laurence's cell

Enter Friar Laurence and Romeo

Friar Laurence. So smile the heavens upon this holy act
 That after-hours with sorrow chide us not!
Romeo. Amen, amen! but come what sorrow can,
 It cannot countervail the exchange of joy
 That one short minute gives me in her sight:
 Do thou but close our hands with holy words,
 Then love-devouring death do what he dare,
 It is enough I may but call her mine.
Friar Laurence. These violent delights have violent ends,
 And in their triumph die; like fire and powder
 Which as they kiss consume: the sweetest honey
 Is loathsome in his own deliciousness,
 And in the taste confounds the appetite:
 Therefore, love moderately; long love doth so;
 Too swift arrives as tardy as too slow.

Enter Juliet somewhat fast, and embraceth Romeo

 Here comes the lady. O, so light a foot
 Will ne'er wear out the everlasting flint.
 A lover may bestride the gossamers
 That idles in the wanton summer air,
 And yet not fall, so light is vanity.
Juliet. Good even to my ghostly confessor.
Friar Laurence. Romeo shall thank thee, daughter, for us
  both.
Juliet. As much to him, else is his thanks too much.
Romeo. Ah, Juliet, if the measure of thy joy
 Be heap'd like mine, and that thy skill be more
 To blazon it, then sweeten with thy breath
 This neighbour air, and let rich music's tongue
 Unfold the imagin'd happiness that both
 Receive in either by this dear encounter.
Juliet. Conceit, more rich in matter than in words,

Brags of his substance, not of ornament:
They are but beggars that can count their worth;
But my true love is grown to such excess,
I cannot sum up sum of half my wealth.

Friar Laurence. Come, come with me, and we will make
short work;
For, by your leaves, you shall not stay alone
Till holy church incorporate two in one.   *Exeunt*

ACT III

Scene I

A public place

Enter Mercutio, Benvolio, Page, and Servants

Benvolio. I pray thee, good Mercutio, let's retire:
  The day is hot, the Capulets abroad,
  {And, if we meet, we shall not 'scape a brawl,
  For now these hot days is the mad blood stirring.}

Mercutio. Thou art like one of these fellows that when he
  enters the confines of a tavern claps me his rapier on the
  board, and says 'God send me no need of thee!' and by
  the operation of the second cup draws it on the drawer,
  when indeed there is no need.

Benvolio. Am I like such a fellow?

Mercutio. Come, come, thou art as hot a Jack in thy mood
  as any in Italy, and as soon mov'd to be moody, and as
  soon moody to be mov'd.

Benvolio. And what to?

Mercutio. Nay, an there were two such, we should have
  none shortly, for one would kill the other. Thou! why,
  thou wilt quarrel with a man that hath a hair more, or a
  hair less, in his beard than thou hast: thou wilt quarrel
  with a man for cracking nuts, having no other reason but
  because thou hast hazel eyes; what eye, but such an eye,
  would spy out such a quarrel? thy head is as full of quar-
  rels as an egg is full of meat, and yet thy head hath been
  beaten as addle as an egg for quarrelling: thou hast quar-
  relled with a man for coughing in the street, because he
  hath wakened thy dog that hath lain asleep in the sun:
  didst thou not fall out with a tailor for wearing his new
  doublet before Easter? with another, for tying his new

shoes with old riband? and yet thou wilt tutor me from quarrelling!

Benvolio. An I were so apt to quarrel as thou art, any man should buy the fee-simple of my life for an hour and a quarter.

Mercutio. The fee-simple! O simple!

Enter Tybalt and others

Benvolio. By my head, here comes the Capulets.

Mercutio. By my heel, I care not.

Tybalt. Follow me close, for I will speak to them.
Gentlemen, good den: a word with one of you.

Mercutio. And but one word with one of us? couple it with something, make it a word and a blow.

Tybalt. You shall find me apt enough to that, sir, an you will give me occasion.

Mercutio. Could you not take some occasion without giving?

Tybalt. Mercutio, thou consorts with Romeo,—

Mercutio. Consort! what, dost thou make us minstrels? an thou make minstrels of us, look to hear nothing but discords: here's my fiddlestick; here's that shall make you dance. 'Zounds, consort!

Benvolio. We talk here in the public haunt of men:
Either withdraw unto some private place,
Or reason coldly of your grievances,
Or else depart, here all eyes gaze on us.

Mercutio. Men's eyes were made to look, and let them gaze;
I will not budge for no man's pleasure, I.

Enter Romeo

Tybalt. Well, peace be with you, sir, here comes my man.

Mercutio. But I'll be hang'd, sir, if he wear your livery:
Marry, go before to field, he'll be your follower;
Your worship in that sense may call him man.

Tybalt. Romeo, the love I bear thee can afford
No better term than this,—thou art a villain.

Romeo. Tybalt, the reason that I have to love thee
Doth much excuse the appertaining rage

To such a greeting: villain am I none;
Therefore farewell, I see thou know'st me not.
Tybalt. Boy, this shall not excuse the injuries
That thou hast done me, therefore turn and draw.
Romeo. I do protest, I never injur'd thee,
But love thee better than thou canst devise
Till thou shalt know the reason of my love:
And so, good Capulet,—which name I tender
As dearly as mine own,—be satisfied.
Mercutio. O calm, dishonourable, vile submission!
Alla stoccata carries it away.   *Draws*
Tybalt, you rat-catcher, will you walk?
Tybalt. What wouldst thou have with me?
Mercutio. Good king of cats, nothing but one of your nine
lives, that I mean to make bold withal, and, as you shall
use me hereafter, dry-beat the rest of the eight. Will you
pluck your sword out of his pilcher by the ears? make
haste, lest mine be about your ears ere it be out.
Tybalt. I am for you.   *Drawing*
Romeo. Gentle Mercutio, put thy rapier up.
Mercutio. Come, sir, your passado.   *They fight*
Romeo. Draw, Benvolio; beat down their weapons.
Gentlemen, for shame, forbear this outrage!
Tybalt, Mercutio, the prince expressly hath
Forbid this bandying in Verona streets:
Hold, Tybalt! good Mercutio!
                Tybalt under Romeo's arm thrusts Mercutio in,
                            and flies with his followers
Mercutio.   I am hurt;
A plague o' both your houses, I am sped:
Is he gone, and hath nothing?
Benvolio.   What, art thou hurt?
Mercutio. Ay, ay, a scratch, a scratch; marry, 'tis enough.
Where is my page? Go, villain, fetch a surgeon.
                                                Exit Page
Romeo. Courage, man; the hurt cannot be much.
Mercutio. No, 'tis not so deep as a well, nor so wide as a
churchdoor, but 'tis enough, 'twill serve: ask for me to-
morrow, and you shall find me a grave man. I am pep-

per'd, I warrant, for this world. A plague o' both your
houses! 'Zounds, a dog, a rat, a mouse, a cat, to scratch a
man to death! a braggart, a rogue, a villain, that fights by
the book of arithmetic! Why the devil came you between us? I was hurt under your arm.

Romeo. I thought all for the best.

Mercutio. Help me into some house, Benvolio,
Or I shall faint. A plague o' both your houses!
They have made worms' meat of me: I have it,
And soundly too: your houses!

Exeunt Mercutio and Benvolio

Romeo. This gentleman, the prince's near ally,
My very friend, hath ta'en this mortal wound
In my behalf, my reputation stain'd
With Tybalt's slander,—Tybalt, that an hour
Hath been my kinsman: O sweet Juliet,
Thy beauty makes me thus effeminate,
And in my temper softens valour's steel!

Re-enter Benvolio

Benvolio. O Romeo, Romeo, brave Mercutio's dead!
That gallant spirit hath aspir'd the clouds,
Which too untimely scorn'd the lowly earth.

Romeo. This day's black fate on more days doth depend;
This but begins the woe others must end.

Re-enter Tybalt

Benvolio. Here comes the furious Tybalt back again.

Romeo. Alive, in triumph, and Mercutio slain?
Away to heaven, respective lenity,
And fire-eyed fury be my conduct now!
Now, Tybalt, take the 'villain' back again
That late thou gav'st me, for Mercutio's soul
Is but a little way above our heads,
And stays for thine to bear him company:
Or thou, or I, or both, shall follow him.

{*Tybalt.* Thou, wretched boy, that didst consort him here,
Shalt with him hence.

Romeo.   This shall determine that.}

                            They fight; Tybalt falls

Benvolio. Romeo, away, be gone!
    The citizens are up, and Tybalt slain:
    Stand not amaz'd: the prince will doom thee death
    If thou art taken: hence, be gone, away!
Romeo. O, I am fortune's fool!
Benvolio.   Why dost thou stay?

                              Exit Romeo

          Enter Citizens, &c.

First Cit. Which way ran he that kill'd Mercutio?
    Tybalt, that murderer, which way ran he?
Benvolio. There lies that Tybalt.
First Cit.   Up, sir, go with me;
    I charge thee in the prince's name, obey.

     Enter Prince, attended; Montague, Capulet, their Wives,
                and others

Escalus. Where are the vile beginners of this fray?
Benvolio. O noble prince, I can discover all
    The unlucky manage of this fatal brawl:
    There lies the man, slain by young Romeo,
    That slew thy kinsman, brave Mercutio.
Lady Capulet. Tybalt, my cousin! O my brother's child!
    O prince! O cousin! husband! O, the blood is spilt
    Of my dear kinsman! Prince, as thou art true,
    For blood of ours, shed blood of Montague.
    O cousin, cousin!
Escalus. Benvolio, who began this bloody fray?
Benvolio. Tybalt, here slain, whom Romeo's hand did slay;
    Romeo that spoke him fair, bid him bethink
    How nice the quarrel was, and urg'd withal
    Your high displeasure: all this uttered
    With gentle breath, calm look, knees humbly bow'd,
    Could not take truce with the unruly spleen
    Of Tybalt deaf to peace, but that he tilts
    With piercing steel at bold Mercutio's breast;
    Who, all as hot, turns deadly point to point,

And, with a martial scorn, with one hand beats
Cold death aside, and with the other sends
It back to Tybalt, whose dexterity
Retorts it: Romeo he cries aloud,
'Hold, friends! friends, part!' and swifter than his tongue,
His agile arm beats down their fatal points,
And 'twixt them rushes; underneath whose arm
An envious thrust from Tybalt hit the life
Of stout Mercutio, and then Tybalt fled,
But by and by comes back to Romeo,
Who had but newly entertain'd revenge,
And to 't they go like lightning, for, ere I
Could draw to part them, was stout Tybalt slain;
And, as he fell, did Romeo turn and fly;
This is the truth, or let Benvolio die.

Lady Capulet. He is a kinsman of the Montague,
Affection makes him false, he speaks not true:
Some twenty of them fought in this black strife,
And all those twenty could but kill one life.
I beg for justice, which thou, prince, must give;
Romeo slew Tybalt, Romeo must not live.

Escalus. Romeo slew him, he slew Mercutio;
Who now the price of his dear blood doth owe?

Montague. Not Romeo, prince, he was Mercutio's friend;
His fault concludes but what the law should end,
The life of Tybalt.

Escalus.   And for that offence
Immediately we do exile him hence:
I have an interest in your hate's proceeding,
My blood for your rude brawls doth lie a-bleeding;
But I'll amerce you with so strong a fine,
That you shall all repent the loss of mine:
I will be deaf to pleading and excuses;
Nor tears nor prayers shall purchase out abuses:
{Therefore use none: let Romeo hence in haste,
Else, when he's found, that hour is his last.}
Bear hence this body, and attend our will:
Mercy but murders, pardoning those that kill.

Exeunt

Scene II

Capulet's orchard

Enter Juliet

Juliet. Gallop apace, you fiery-footed steeds,
  Towards Phœbus' lodging: such a waggoner
  As Phaethon would whip you to the west,
  And bring in cloudy night immediately.
  {Spread thy close curtain, love-performing night,
  That runaways' eyes may wink, and Romeo
  Leap to these arms, untalk'd of and unseen.
  Lovers can see to do their amorous rites
  By their own beauties, or, if love be blind,
  It best agrees with night. Come, civil night,
  Thou sober-suited matron, all in black,
  And learn me how to lose a winning match,
  Play'd for a pair of stainless maidenhoods:
  Hood my unmann'd blood bating in my cheeks
  With thy black mantle, till strange love grow bold,
  Think true love acted simple modesty.
  Come night, come Romeo, come, thou day in night;
  For thou wilt lie upon the wings of night
  Whiter than new snow on a raven's back.
  Come, gentle night, come, loving, black-brow'd night,
  Give me my Romeo; and, when he shall die,
  Take him and cut him out in little stars,
  And he will make the face of heaven so fine,
  That all the world will be in love with night,
  And pay no worship to the garish sun.
  O, I have bought the mansion of a love,
  But not possess'd it, and, though I am sold.
  Not yet enjoy'd; so tedious is this day
  As is the night before some festival
  To an impatient child that hath new robes
  And may not wear them. O, here comes my nurse,
  And she brings news, and every tongue that speaks
  But Romeo's name speaks heavenly eloquence.}

Enter Nurse wringing her hands, with the ladder of cords

Now, nurse, what news? What hast thou there? the cords
That Romeo bid thee fetch?
Nurse.   Ay, ay, the cords.
Juliet. Ay me! what news? why dost thou wring thy hands?
Nurse. Ah, well-a-day! he's dead, he's dead, he's dead.
   We are undone, lady, we are undone.
   Alack the day! he's gone, he's kill'd, he's dead.
Juliet. Can heaven be so envious?
Nurse.   Romeo can,
   Though heaven cannot. O Romeo, Romeo!
   Who ever would have thought it? Romeo!
Juliet. What devil art thou that dost torment me thus?
   This torture should be roar'd in dismal hell.
   {Hath Romeo slain himself? say thou but 'Ay,'
   And that bare vowel 'I' shall poison more
   Than the death-darting eye of cockatrice:
   I am not I, if there be such an Ay,
   Or those eyes shut, that make thee answer 'Ay.'
   If he be slain, say 'Ay;' or if not, No:
   Brief sounds determine of my weal or woe.}
Nurse. I saw the wound, I saw it with mine eyes—
   God save the mark!—here on his manly breast:
   A piteous corse, a bloody piteous corse;
   Pale, pale as ashes, {all bedaub'd in blood,
   All in gore blood:} I swounded at the sight.
Juliet. O, break, my heart! poor bankrupt, break at once!
   To prison, eyes, ne'er look on liberty!
   Vile earth, to earth resign, end motion here,
   And thou and Romeo press one heavy bier!
Nurse. O Tybalt, Tybalt, the best friend I had!
   O courteous Tybalt! honest gentleman!
   {That ever I should live to see thee dead!}
Juliet. What storm is this that blows so contrary?
   Is Romeo slaughter'd, and is Tybalt dead?
   My dear-lov'd cousin, and my dearer lord?
   Then, dreadful trumpet, sound the general doom!
   For who is living, if those two are gone?

Nurse. Tybalt is gone, and Romeo banished;
  Romeo that murder'd him is banished.
Juliet. O God! did Romeo's hand shed Tybalt's blood?
Nurse. It did, it did; alas the day, it did!
Juliet. O serpent heart, hid with a flowering face!
  {Did ever dragon keep so fair a cave?
  Beautiful tyrant! fiend angelical!
  Dove-feather'd raven! wolvish-ravening lamb!
  Despised substance of divinest show!
  Just opposite to what thou justly seem'st,
  A damned saint, an honourable villain!
  O nature, what hadst thou to do in hell,
  When thou didst bower the spirit of a fiend
  In mortal paradise of such sweet flesh?}
  Was ever book containing such vile matter
  So fairly bound? O, that deceit should dwell
  In such a gorgeous palace!
Nurse.   There's no trust,
  No faith, no honesty in men; all perjur'd,
  All forsworn, all naught, all dissemblers.
  {Ah, where's my man? give me some aqua vitæ:
  These griefs, these woes, these sorrows make me old.}
  Shame come to Romeo!
Juliet.   Blister'd be thy tongue
  For such a wish! he was not born to shame:
  Upon his brow shame is asham'd to sit;
  {For 'tis a throne where honour may be crown'd
  Sole monarch of the universal earth.
  O, what a beast was I to chide at him!
Nurse. Will you speak well of him that kill'd your cousin?
Juliet. Shall I speak ill of him that is my husband?
  Ah, poor my lord, what tongue shall smooth thy name,
  When I, thy three-hours wife, have mangled it?}
  But wherefore, villain, didst thou kill my cousin?
  That villain cousin would have kill'd my husband:
  {Back, foolish tears, back to your native spring;
  Your tributary drops belong to woe,
  Which you mistaking offer up to joy.
  My husband lives, that Tybalt would have slain;

And Tybalt's dead, that would have slain my husband:}
All this is comfort, wherefore weep I then?
Some word there was, worser than Tybalt's death,
That murder'd me: I would forget it fain,
But, O, it presses to my memory,
{Like damned guilty deeds to sinners' minds:
'Tybalt is dead, and Romeo banished;'
That 'banished,' that one word 'banished,'
Hath slain ten thousand Tybalts. Tybalt's death
Was woe enough, if it had ended there:
Or, if sour woe delights in fellowship,
And needly will be rank'd with other griefs,
Why follow'd not, when she said 'Tybalt's dead,'
Thy father, or thy mother, nay, or both,
Which modern lamentation might have mov'd?
But with a rear-ward following Tybalt's death,}
'Romeo is banished:' to speak that word,
Is father, mother, Tybalt, Romeo, Juliet,
All slain, all dead. {'Romeo is banished.'
There is no end, no limit, measure, bound,
In that word's death; no words can that woe sound.}
Where is my father, and my mother, nurse?
Nurse. Weeping and wailing over Tybalt's corse:
 Will you go to them? I will bring you thither.
Juliet. Wash they his wounds with tears? mine shall be
   spent,
 When theirs are dry, for Romeo's banishment.
 {Take up those cords: poor ropes, you are beguil'd,
 Both you and I; for Romeo is exil'd:
 He made you for a highway to my bed,
 But I, a maid, die maiden widowed.
 Come cords, come nurse, I'll to my wedding-bed;
 And death, not Romeo, take my maidenhead!
Nurse. Hie to your chamber, I'll find Romeo
 To comfort you, I wot well where he is.}
 Hark ye, your Romeo will be here at night,
 I'll to him, he is hid at Laurence' cell.
Juliet. O, find him! give this ring to my true knight,
 And bid him come, to take his last farewell.   *Exeunt*

Scene III

Friar Laurence's Cell

Enter Friar Laurence

Friar Laurence. Romeo, come forth, come forth, thou fearful
    man:
    Affliction is enamour'd of thy parts,
    And thou art wedded to calamity.

Enter Romeo

Romeo. Father, what news? what is the prince's doom?
    What sorrow craves acquaintance at my hand,
    That I yet know not?
Friar Laurence.   Too familiar
    Is my young son with such sour company:
    I bring thee tidings of the prince's doom.
Romeo. What less than dooms-day is the prince's doom?
Friar Laurence. A gentler judgement vanish'd from his lips,
    Not body's death, but body's banishment.
Romeo. Ha, banishment? be merciful, say 'death;'
    For exile hath more terror in his looks,
    Than death itself: do not say 'banishment.'
Friar Laurence. Hence from Verona art thou banished:
    Be patient, for the world is broad and wide.
Romeo. There is no world without Verona walls,
    But purgatory, torture, hell itself.
    Hence banished is banish'd from the world,
    And world's exile is death: {then 'banished'
    Is death mis-term'd:} calling death 'banished,'
    Thou cut'st my head off with a golden axe,
    And smilest upon the stroke that murders me.
Friar Laurence. O monstrous sin! O rude unthankfulness!
    Thy fault our law calls death, but the mild prince,
    Taking thy part, hath rush'd aside the law,
    And turn'd that black word death to banishment:
    This is mere mercy, and thou seest it not.
Romeo. 'Tis torture, and not mercy: heaven is here,

Where Juliet lives; and every cat and dog
And little mouse, every unworthy thing,
Live here in heaven, and may look on her,
But Romeo may not: more validity,
More honourable state, more courtship lives
In carrion-flies than Romeo: they may seize
On the white wonder of dear Juliet's skin,
And steal immortal kisses from her lips,
{Who, even in pure and vestal modesty,
Still blush, as thinking their own kisses sin;}
But Romeo may not; he is banished:
This may flies do, but I from this must fly:
{They are free men, but I am banished:
And say'st thou yet, that exile is not death?}
Hadst thou no poison mix'd, no sharp-ground knife,
No present mean of death, though ne'er so mean,
But 'banished' to kill me?—'Banished'?
O friar, the damned use that word in hell;
Howling attends it: how hadst thou the heart,
Being a divine, a ghostly confessor,
A sin-absolver, and my friend profess'd,
To mangle me with that word 'banished'?

Friar Laurence. Thou fond mad man, hear me but speak a
    word.

Romeo. O, thou wilt talk again of banishment.

Friar Laurence. I'll give thee armour to keep off that word;
    Adversity's sweet milk, philosophy,
    To comfort thee, though thou be banished.

Romeo. Yet 'banished'? Hang up philosophy,
    Unless philosophy can make a Juliet,
    Displant a town, reverse a prince's doom,
    It helps not, it prevails not, talk no more.

Friar Laurence. O, then I see that madmen have no ears.

Romeo. How should they, when that wise men have no
    eyes?

Friar Laurence. Let me dispute with thee of thy estate.

Romeo. Thou canst not speak of what thou dost not feel:
    Wert thou as young as I, Juliet thy love,
    An hour but married, Tybalt murdered,

Doting like me, and like me banished,
Then mightst thou speak, then mightst thou tear thy hair,
And fall upon the ground, as I do now,
Taking the measure of an unmade grave.

Knocking within

Friar Laurence. Arise, one knocks; good Romeo, hide thy-
self.
{*Romeo.* Not I; unless the breath of heart-sick groans
Mist-like infold me from the search of eyes.

Knocking

Friar Laurence. Hark, how they knock! Who's there? Romeo, arise;
Thou wilt be taken.—Stay awhile!—Stand up;

Knocking

Run to my study.—By and by!—God's will,
What simpleness is this!—I come, I come!

Knocking

Who knocks so hard? whence come you? what's your
will?}
Nurse. (*within*) Let me come in, and you shall know my er-
rand;
I come from Lady Juliet.
Friar Laurence.   Welcome then.

Enter Nurse

Nurse. O holy friar, O, tell me, holy friar,
Where is my lady's lord, where's Romeo?
Friar Laurence. There on the ground, with his own tears
made drunk.
Nurse. O, he is even in my mistress' case,
Just in her case!
Friar Laurence.   O woeful sympathy!
Piteous predicament!
Nurse.   Even so lies she,
Blubbering and weeping, weeping and blubbering.
Stand up, stand up, stand, an you be a man:
For Juliet's sake, for her sake, rise and stand;
Why should you fall into so deep an O?   *He rises*
Romeo. Nurse!

Nurse. Ah sir! ah sir! Well, death's the end of all.

Romeo. Spakest thou of Juliet? how is it with her?
　Doth she not think me an old murderer,
　Now I have stain'd the childhood of her joy
　With blood remov'd but little from her own?
　Where is she? and how doth she? and what says
　My conceal'd lady to our cancell'd love?

Nurse. O, she says nothing, sir, but weeps and pules;
　And now falls on her bed; and then starts up,
　And Tybalt calls; and then on Romeo cries,
　And then down falls again.

Romeo.　　　　　　　　　As if that name,
　Shot from the deadly level of a gun,
　Did murder her, as that name's cursed hand
　Murder'd her kinsman. O, tell me, friar, tell me,
　In what vile part of this anatomy
　Doth my name lie? tell me, that I may sack
　The hateful mansion.

　　　　　　　He offers to stab himself, and the Nurse
　　　　　　　　　snatches the dagger away

Friar Laurence.　　　　　Hold thy desperate hand:
　Art thou a man? thy form cries out thou art:
　Thy tears are womanish; thy wild acts denote
　The unreasonable fury of a beast:
　Unseemly woman in a seeming man,
　Or ill-beseeming beast in seeming both!
　Thou hast amaz'd me: by my holy order,
　I thought thy disposition better temper'd.
　Hast thou slain Tybalt? wilt thou slay thyself?
　And slay thy lady too that lives in thee,
　{By doing damned hate upon thyself?
　Why rail'st thou on thy birth, the heaven and earth?
　Since birth, and heaven, and earth, all three do meet
　In thee at once, which thou at once wouldst lose.
　Fie, fie, thou sham'st thy shape, thy love, thy wit,
　Which, like a usurer, abound'st in all,
　And usest none in that true use indeed
　Which should bedeck thy shape, thy love, thy wit:
　Thy noble shape is but a form of wax,

Digressing from the valour of a man;
Thy dear love sworn, but hollow perjury,
Killing that love which thou hast vow'd to cherish;
Thy wit, that ornament to shape and love,
Mis-shapen in the conduct of them both,
Like powder in a skilless soldier's flask,
Is set a-fire by thine own ignorance,
And thou dismember'd with thine own defence.}
What, rouse thee, man! thy Juliet is alive,
For whose dear sake thou wast but lately dead;
There art thou happy: Tybalt would kill thee,
But thou slew'st Tybalt; there art thou happy too:
{The law, that threaten'd death, becomes thy friend,
And turns it to exile; there art thou happy:}
A pack of blessings lights upon thy back,
Happiness courts thee in her best array,
But, like a misbehav'd and sullen wench,
Thou frown'st upon thy fate that smiles on thee:
Take heed, take heed, for such die miserable.
Go, get thee to thy love, as was decreed,
Ascend her chamber, hence and comfort her:
{But look thou stay not till the watch be set,
For then thou canst not pass to Mantua;
Where thou shalt live till we can find a time
To blaze your marriage, reconcile your friends,
Beg pardon of the prince, and call thee back
With twenty hundred thousand times more joy
Than thou went'st forth in lamentation.}
Go before, nurse: commend me to thy lady,
And bid her hasten all the house to bed,
Which heavy sorrow makes them apt unto:
{Romeo is coming.}
Nurse. O Lord, I could have stay'd here all the night
To hear good counsel: O, what learning is!
My lord, I'll tell my lady you will come.
Romeo. Do so, and bid my sweet prepare to chide.

Nurse offers to go in and turns again

Nurse. Here, sir, a ring she bid me give you, sir:
{Hie you, make haste, for it grows very late.}   *Exit*

Romeo. How well my comfort is reviv'd by this!

Friar Laurence. Go hence, good night, and here stands all
  your state:
 Either be gone before the watch be set,
 Or by the break of day disguis'd from hence:}
 Sojourn in Mantua; I'll find out your man,
 And he shall signify from time to time
 Every good hap to you that chances here:
 {Give me thy hand, 'tis late,} farewell, {good night.}

Romeo. But that a joy past joy calls out on me,
 It were a grief, so brief to part with thee:
 {Farewell.}   *Exeunt*

Scene IV

A room in Capulet's house

Enter Capulet, Lady Capulet, and Paris

Capulet. Things have fall'n out, sir, so unluckily,
 That we have had no time to move our daughter.
 Look you, she lov'd her kinsman Tybalt dearly,
 And so did I. Well, we were born to die.
 'Tis very late; she'll not come down to-night:
 I promise you, but for your company,
 I would have been a-bed an hour ago.

Paris. These times of woe afford no times to woo.
 Madam, good night, commend me to your daughter.

{*Lady Capulet.* I will, and know her mind early to-morrow;
 To-night she's mew'd up to her heaviness.}

Capulet. Sir Paris, I will make a desperate tender
 Of my child's love: I think she will be rul'd
 In all respects by me; nay more, I doubt it not.
 Wife, go you to her ere you go to bed;
 Acquaint her here of my son Paris' love;
 And bid her, mark you me, on Wednesday next—
 But, soft! what day is this?

Paris.   Monday, my lord.

Capulet. {Monday! ha, ha!} Well, Wednesday is too soon;
 O' Thursday let it be: o' Thursday, tell her,

{She shall be married to this noble earl.
Will you be ready? do you like this haste?}
We'll keep no great ado; a friend or two;
For, hark you, Tybalt being slain so late,
It will be thought we held him carelessly,
Being our kinsman, if we revel much:
Therefore we'll have some half-a-dozen friends,
And there an end. But what say you to Thursday?
Paris. My lord, I would that Thursday were to-morrow.
Capulet. Well, you get gone: o' Thursday be it then.
Go you to Juliet ere you go to bed,
Prepare her, wife, against this wedding-day.
Farewell, my lord. Light to my chamber, ho!
Afore me, it is so very very late,
That we may call it early by and by:
Good night.   *Exeunt*

Scene V

Capulet's orchard

Enter Romeo and Juliet, above, at the window

Juliet. Wilt thou be gone? it is not yet near day:
It was the nightingale, and not the lark,
That pierc'd the fearful hollow of thine ear;
Nightly she sings on yond pomegranate-tree:
Believe me, love, it was the nightingale.
Romeo. It was the lark, the herald of the morn,
No nightingale: look, love, what envious streaks
Do lace the severing clouds in yonder east:
Night's candles are burnt out, and jocund day
Stands tiptoe on the misty mountain tops:
I must be gone and live, or stay and die.
Juliet. Yond light is not day-light, I know it, I:
It is some meteor that the sun exhales,
To be to thee this night a torch-bearer,
And light thee on thy way to Mantua:
Therefore stay awhile, thou shalt not go so soon.
Romeo. Let me stay here, let me be ta'en, and die;

I am content, so thou wilt have it so.
I'll say yon grey is not the morning's eye,
'Tis but the pale reflex of Cynthia's brow;
I'll say it is the nightingale that beats
The vaulty heaven so high above our heads,
And not the lark, the messenger of morn.
I have more care to stay than will to go:
Come, death, and welcome! Juliet wills it so.
What says my love? let's talk: 'tis not yet day.
Juliet. It is, it is: be gone, fly hence, away!
It is the lark that sings so out of tune,
Straining harsh discords and unpleasing sharps.
Some say the lark makes sweet division;
This doth not so, for this divideth us:
Some say the lark and loathed toad change eyes;
I would that now they had changed voices too!
Since arm from arm her voice doth us affray,
Hunting thee hence with hunts-up to the day.
So now be gone, more light and light it grows.
Romeo. More light and light: more dark and dark our woes!

Enter Nurse, to the chamber

Nurse. Madam!
Juliet. Nurse?
Nurse. Your lady mother is coming to your chamber:
The day is broke; be wary, look about.   *Exit*
{*Juliet.* Then, window, let day in, and let life out.}
Romeo. Farewell, my love! one kiss, and I'll descend.
                                                                 Descends
Juliet. Art thou gone so? my lord, my love, my friend!
I must hear from thee every day in the hour,
For in an hour there are many minutes,
Minutes are days, so I will number them:
O, by this count I shall be much in years
Ere I see thee again!
Romeo. Farewell!
I will omit no opportunity
That may convey my greetings, love, to thee.
Juliet. O, think'st thou we shall ever meet again?

Romeo. No doubt, no doubt; and all these woes shall serve
 For sweet discourses in our time to come.
Juliet. O God! I have an ill-divining soul.
 Methinks I see thee, now thou art below,
 As one dead in the bottom of a tomb:
 Either my eyesight fails or thou look'st pale.
Romeo. And trust me, love, in my eye so do you:
 Dry sorrow drinks our blood. Adieu, adieu!   *Exit*
{*Juliet.* O fortune, fortune! all men call thee fickle:
 If thou art fickle, what dost thou with him
 That is renown'd for faith? Be fickle, fortune;
 For then, I hope, thou wilt not keep him long,
 But send him back.}
Lady Capulet. (*within*) Ho, daughter! are you up?
Juliet. Who is 't that calls? {it is my lady mother!
 Is she not down so late, or up so early?
 What unaccustom'd cause procures her hither?}

Enter Lady Capulet

Lady Capulet. Why, how now, Juliet!
Juliet.   Madam, I am not well.
Lady Capulet. Evermore weeping for your cousin's death?
 What, wilt thou wash him from his grave with tears?
 {An if thou couldst, thou couldst not make him live;
 Therefore have done: some grief shows much of love,
 But much of grief shows still some want of wit.}
Juliet. Yet let me weep for such a feeling loss.
{*Lady Capulet.* So shall you feel the loss, but not the friend
 Which you weep for.
Juliet.   Feeling so the loss,
 I cannot choose but ever weep the friend.}
Lady Capulet. Well, girl, thou weep'st not so much for his
  death
 As that the villain lives which slaughter'd him.
Juliet. What villain, madam?
Lady Capulet.   That same villain, Romeo.
Juliet. (*aside*) Villain and he are many miles asunder.
 {God pardon him! I do, with all my heart;
 And yet no man like he doth grieve my heart.}

Lady Capulet. That is because the traitor murderer lives.
Juliet. Ay, madam, from the reach of these my hands:
    Would none but I might venge my cousin's death!
Lady Capulet. We will have vengeance for it, fear thou not:
    Then weep no more.} I'll send to one in Mantua,
    Where that same banish'd runagate doth live,
    Shall give him such an unaccustom'd dram
    That he shall soon keep Tybalt company:
    And then, I hope, thou wilt be satisfied.
Juliet. Indeed, I never shall be satisfied
    With Romeo, till I behold him—dead—
    Is my poor heart so for a kinsman vex'd.
    {Madam, if you could find out but a man
    To bear a poison, I would temper it,
    That Romeo should, upon receipt thereof,
    Soon sleep in quiet. O, how my heart abhors
    To hear him named, and cannot come to him,
    To wreak the love I bore my cousin
    Upon his body that hath slaughter'd him!}
Lady Capulet. {Find thou the means, and I'll find such a
    man.}
    But now I'll tell thee joyful tidings, girl.
Juliet. And joy comes well in such a needy time:
    {What are they, I beseech your ladyship?}
Lady Capulet. Well then, thou hast a careful father, girl;
    One who, to put thee from thy heaviness,
    Hath sorted out a sudden day of joy,
    {That thou expect'st not, nor I look'd not for.}
Juliet. Madam, in happy time, what day is that?
Lady Capulet. Marry, my child, early next Thursday morn,
    The gallant, young, and noble gentleman,
    The County Paris, at Saint Peter's Church,
    Shall happily make thee there a joyful bride.
Juliet. Now, by Saint Peter's Church, and Peter too,
    He shall not make me there a joyful bride.
    {I wonder at this haste, that I must wed
    Ere he that should be husband comes to woo.
    I pray you, tell my lord and father, madam,}
    I will not marry yet; and, when I do, I swear,

It shall be rather Romeo, whom I hate,
Than County Paris whom I cannot love.

Lady Capulet. Here comes your father; tell him so yourself,
{And see how he will take it at your hands.}

Enter Capulet and Nurse

Capulet. {When the sun sets, the air doth drizzle dew;
But for the sunset of my brother's son
It rains downright.}
How now? a conduit, girl? what, still in tears?
Evermore showering? In one little body
Thou counterfeit'st a bark, a sea, a wind:
For still thy eyes, which I may call the sea,
Do ebb and flow with tears, the bark thy body is,
Sailing in this salt flood, the winds, thy sighs,
Who raging with thy tears, and they with them,
Without a sudden calm will overset
Thy tempest-tossed body. How now, wife?
Have you deliver'd to her our decree?

Lady Capulet. Ay, sir, but she will none, she gives you
thanks.
I would the fool were married to her grave!

Capulet. Soft! take me with you, take me with you, wife.
How? will she none? doth she not give us thanks?
Is she not proud? {doth she not count her blest,
Unworthy as she is, that we have wrought
So worthy a gentleman to be her bridegroom?}

Juliet. Not proud you have, but thankful that you have:
Proud can I never be of that I hate;
But thankful even for hate that is meant love.

Capulet. How, how! how, how! chop-logic! What is this?
'Proud,' and 'I thank you,' and 'I thank you not;'
And yet 'not proud:' mistress minion, you,
Thank me no thankings, nor proud me no prouds,
But fettle your fine joints on Thursday next,
To go with Paris to Saint Peter's Church,
Or I will drag thee on a hurdle thither.
Out, you green-sickness carrion! out, you baggage!

You tallow-facc!

{Lady Capulet.   Fie, fie! what, are you mad?}

Juliet. Good father, I beseech you on my knees,
    Hear me with patience but to speak a word.

Capulet. {Hang thee, young baggage! disobedient wretch!}
    I tell thee what, get thee to church o' Thursday,
    Or never after look me in the face:
    Speak not, reply not, do not answer me;
    My fingers itch. Wife, we scarce thought us blest
    That God had lent us but this only child;
    But now I see this one is one too much,
    And that we have a cross in having her:
    {Out on her, hilding!}

Nurse.   God in heaven bless her!
    You are to blame, my lord, to rate her so.

Capulet. And why, my lady wisdom? hold your tongue,
    Good prudence; smatter with your gossips, go.

Nurse. I speak no treason.

Capulet.   O, God ye god-den.

{Nurse. May not one speak?

Capulet.   Peace, you mumbling fool!}
    Utter your gravity o'er a gossip's bowl;
    For here we need it not.

Lady Capulet.   You are too hot.

Capulet. God's bread! it makes me mad:
    Day, night, hour, tide, time, work, play,
    Alone, in company, still my care hath been
    To have her match'd, and having now provided
    A gentleman of noble parentage,
    Of fair demesnes, youthful, and nobly train'd,
    Stuff'd, as they say, with honourable parts,
    Proportion'd as one's heart could wish a man;
    And then to have a wretched puling fool,
    A whining mammet, in her fortune's tender,
    To answer 'I'll not wed; I cannot love,
    I am too young; I pray you, pardon me.'
    But, an you will not wed, I'll pardon you:
    Graze where you will, you shall not house with me:
    Look to 't, think on 't, I do not use to jest.

Thursday is near; lay hand on heart, advise:
An you be mine, I'll give you to my friend;
An you be not, hang, beg, starve, die in the streets,
For, by my soul, I'll ne'er acknowledge thee,
Nor what is mine shall never do thee good:
Trust to 't, bethink you; I'll not be forsworn.   *Exit*

Juliet. Is there no pity sitting in the clouds,
That sees into the bottom of my grief?
O, sweet my mother, cast me not away!
Delay this marriage for a month, a week;
Or, if you do not, make my marriage bed
In that dim monument where Tybalt lies.

Lady Capulet. Talk not to me, for I'll not speak a word:
Do as thou wilt, for I have done with thee.   *Exit*

Juliet. O God!—O nurse, {how shall this be prevented?
My husband is on earth, my faith in heaven,
How shall that faith return again to earth,
Unless that husband send it me from heaven,
By leaving earth?} comfort me, counsel me.
{Alack, alack, that heaven should practise stratagems
Upon so soft a subject as myself!
What say'st thou? hast thou not a word of joy?
Some comfort, nurse.}

Nurse.   Faith, here it is.
Romeo is banish'd, and all the world to nothing,
That he dares ne'er come back to challenge you;
{Or, if he do, it needs must be by stealth.
Then, since the case so stands as now it doth,}
I think it best you married with the county.
O, he's a lovely gentleman!
Romeo's a dishclout to him: {an eagle, madam,
Hath not so green, so quick, so fair an eye
As Paris hath.} Beshrew my very heart,
I think you are happy in this second match,
For it excels your first, or if it did not,
Your first is dead, or 'twere as good he were
As living here and you no use of him.

Juliet. Speakest thou from thy heart?

Nurse.   And from my soul too;
  Else beshrew them both.
Juliet.   Amen!
Nurse.   What?
Juliet. Well, thou hast comforted me marvellous much.
  Go in, and tell my lady I am gone,
  Having displeas'd my father, to Laurence' cell,
  To make confession, and to be absolv'd.
Nurse. Marry, I will, and this is wisely done.   *Exit*
Juliet. Ancient damnation! O most cursed fiend!
  Is it more sin to wish me thus forsworn,
  Or to dispraise my lord with that same tongue
  That thou hath prais'd him with above compare
  So many thousand times? Go, counsellor;
  Thou and my bosom henceforth shall be twain.
  I'll to the friar, to know his remedy:
  If all fail else, I have the power to die.   *Exit*

ACT IV

Scene I

Friar Laurence's cell

Enter Friar Laurence and Paris

Friar Laurence. On Thursday sir? the time is very short.
Paris. My father Capulet will have it so,
   And I am nothing slow to slack his haste.
Friar Laurence. You say you do not know the lady's mind?
   Uneven is the course, I like it not.
Paris. Immoderately she weeps for Tybalt's death,
   And therefore have I little talk'd of love,
   For Venus smiles not in a house of tears.
   Now, sir, her father counts it dangerous
   That she doth give her sorrow so much sway;
   And in his wisdom hastes our marriage,
   To stop the inundation of her tears,
   Which, too much minded by herself alone,
   May be put from her by society:
   Now do you know the reason of this haste.
Friar Laurence. (*aside*) I would I knew not why it should
   be slow'd.
   Look, sir, here comes the lady towards my cell.

Enter Juliet

Paris. Welcome, my love, my lady and my wife!
Juliet. That may be, sir, when I may be a wife.
Paris. That "may be" must be, love, on Thursday next.
Juliet. What must be shall be.
Friar Laurence.   That's a certain text.
Paris. Come you to make confession to this friar?
Juliet. To tell you that were to confess to you.
Paris. Do not deny to him that you love me.
Juliet. I will confess to you that I love him.

Paris. So I am sure you will that you love me.

Juliet. An if I do, it will be of more price,
    Being spoke behind your back, than to your face.

Paris. Poor soul, thy face is much abus'd with tears.

Juliet. The tears have got small victory by that:
    For it was bad enough before their spite.

Paris. Thou wrong'st it more than tears by that report.

Juliet. That is no slander, sir, which is a truth,
    And what I spake, I spake it to my face.

Paris. Thy face is mine, and thou hast slander'd it.

Juliet. It may be so, for it is not mine own.
    Are you at leisure, holy father, now;
    Or shall I come to you at evening mass?

Friar Laurence. My leisure serves me, pensive daughter,
    now.
    My lord, we must entreat the time alone.

Paris. God shield I should disturb devotion:
    Juliet, {on Thursday early will I rouse ye:
    Till then,} adieu, and keep this holy kiss.   *Exit*

Juliet. Go shut the door, and when thou hast done so,
    Come weep with me; past hope, past cure, past help!

Friar Laurence. Ah, Juliet, I already know thy grief;
    {It strains me past the compass of my wits:}
    I hear thou must, and nothing may prorogue it,
    On Thursday next be married to this county.

Juliet. Tell me not, friar, that thou hear'st of this,
    Unless thou tell me how we may prevent it:
    {If in thy wisdom thou canst give no help,
    Do thou but call my resolution wise,
    And with this knife I'll help it presently.
    God join'd my heart and Romeo's, thou our hands;
    And ere this hand, by thee to Romeo's seal'd,
    Shall be the label to another deed,
    Or my true heart with treacherous revolt
    Turn to another, this shall slay them both:
    Therefore, out of thy long-experienc'd time,}
    Give me some present counsel; or, behold,
    'Twixt my extremes and me this bloody knife
    Shall play the umpire, arbitrating that

Which the commission of thy years and art
Could to no issue of true honour bring.
Be not so long to speak; I long to die,
If what thou speak'st speak not of remedy.
Friar Laurence. Hold, daughter, I do spy a kind of hope,
Which craves as desperate an execution
As that is desperate we would prevent.
If, rather than to marry County Paris,
Thou hast the strength of will to slay thyself,
'Tis not unlike that thou wilt undertake
A thing like death to chide away this shame,
That cop'st with death himself to 'scape from it;
And, if thou dar'st, I'll give thee remedy.
Juliet. O, bid me leap, rather than marry Paris,
From off the battlements of yonder tower;
Or walk in thievish ways, or bid me lurk
Where serpents are; chain me with roaring bears;
Or shut me nightly in a charnel-house,
{O'er-cover'd quite with dead men's rattling bones,}
With reeky shanks and yellow chapless skulls;
Or bid me go into a new-made grave,
And hide me with a dead man in his shroud;
Things that to hear them told, have made me tremble;
And I will do it without fear or doubt,
To live an unstain'd wife to my sweet love.
Friar Laurence. {Hold, then, go home, be merry, give
    consent
To marry Paris: Wednesday is to-morrow;}
To-morrow night look that thou lie alone,
Let not thy nurse lie with thee in thy chamber:
Take thou this vial, being then in bed,
And this distilled liquor drink thou off:
When presently through all thy veins shall run
A cold and drowsy humour; for no pulse
Shall keep his native progress, but surcease:
No warmth, no breath, shall testify thou livest;
{The roses in thy lips and cheeks shall fade
To paly ashes; thy eyes' windows fall,

Like death, when he shuts up the day of life;
Each part, deprived of supple government,
Shall, stiff and stark and cold, appear like death}
And in this borrow'd likeness of shrunk death
Thou shalt continue two and forty hours,
{And then awake as from a pleasant sleep.
Now, when the bridegroom in the morning comes
To rouse thee from thy bed, there art thou dead
Then, as the manner of our country is,
In thy best robes uncover'd on the bier}
Thou shalt be borne to that same ancient vault
Where all the kindred of the Capulets lie.
In the mean time, against thou shalt awake,
Shall Romeo by my letters know our drift;
And hither shall he come: and he and I
Will watch thy waking, and that very night
Shall Romeo bear thee hence to Mantua.
{And this shall free thee from this present shame,
If no inconstant toy nor womanish fear
Abate thy valour in the acting it.}

Juliet. Give me, give me! O, tell not me of fear!

Friar Laurence. Hold; get you gone, be strong and pros-
    perous
    In this resolve: I'll send a friar with speed
    To Mantua, with my letters to thy lord.

Juliet. Love give me strength! and strength shall help afford.
    Farewell, dear father!   *Exeunt*

Scene II

Hall in Capulet's house

Enter Capulet, Lady Capulet, Nurse, and two Servingmen

Capulet. So many guests invite as here are writ.

Exit First Servant

Sirrah, go hire me twenty cunning cooks.

Sec. Serv. You shall have none ill, sir, for I'll try if they can
lick their fingers.

Capulet. How canst thou try them so?

Sec. Serv. Marry, sir, 'tis an ill cook that cannot lick his own
fingers: therefore he that cannot lick his fingers goes not
with me.

Capulet. Go, be gone.   *Exit Second Servant*

We shall be much unfurnish'd for this time.

What, is my daughter gone to Friar Laurence?

Nurse. Ay, forsooth.

Capulet. Well, he may chance to do some good on her:
A peevish self-will'd harlotry it is.

Enter Juliet

Nurse. See where she comes from shrift with merry look.

Capulet. How now, my headstrong! where have you been
gadding?

Juliet. Where I have learn'd me to repent the sin
Of froward wilful opposition
'Gainst you and your behests, and am enjoin'd
By holy Laurence to fall prostrate here,
To beg your pardon: pardon, I beseech you!
Henceforward I am ever rul'd by you.

Capulet. Send for the county, go tell him of this,
    I'll have this knot knit up to-morrow morning.
{*Juliet.* I met the youthful lord at Laurence' cell,
    And gave him what becomed love I might,
    Not stepping o'er the bounds of modesty.
Capulet. Why, I am glad on 't, this is well, stand up,
    This is as 't should be. Let me see the county;
    Ay, marry, go, I say, and fetch him hither.}
    Now, afore God, this reverend holy friar,
    All our whole city is much bound to him.
Juliet. Nurse, will you go with me into my closet,
    To help me sort such needful ornaments
    As you think fit to furnish me to-morrow?
Lady Capulet. No, not till Thursday; there is time enough.
Capulet. Go, nurse, go with her: we'll to church to-morrow.
                      Exeunt Juliet and Nurse
Lady Capulet. We shall be short in our provision:
    'Tis now near night.
Capulet.   {Tush, I will stir about,
    And all things shall be well, I warrant thee, wife:}
    Go thou to Juliet, help to deck up her;
    {I'll not to bed to-night, let me alone;
    I'll play the housewife for this once. What, ho!
    They are all forth: well, I will walk myself
    To County Paris, to prepare him up
    Against to-morrow:} my heart is wondrous light,
    Since this same wayward girl is so reclaim'd.   *Exeunt*

Scene III

Juliet's chamber

Enter Juliet and Nurse

Juliet. Ay, those attires are best: but, gentle nurse,
  I pray thee, leave me to myself to-night;
  For I have need of many orisons
  To move the heavens to smile upon my state,
  Which, well thou know'st, is cross and full of sin.

Enter Lady Capulet

Lady Capulet. What, are you busy, ho? need you my help?
Juliet. No, madam; we have cull'd such necessaries
  As are behoveful for our state to-morrow:
  So please you, let me now be left alone,
  And let the nurse this night sit up with you,
  For I am sure you have your hands full all
  In this so sudden business.
Lady Capulet.   Good night:
  Get thee to bed and rest, for thou hast need.
                    Exeunt Lady Capulet and Nurse
Juliet. Farewell! God knows when we shall meet again.
  I have a faint cold fear thrills through my veins,
  That almost freezes up the heat of life:
  I'll call them back again to comfort me.
  Nurse!—What should she do here?
  My dismal scene I needs must act alone.
  Come, vial.
  What if this mixture do not work at all?
  Shall I be married then to-morrow morning?
  No, no: this shall forbid it. Lie thou there.
                    Laying down a dagger

What if it be a poison, which the friar
Subtly hath minister'd to have me dead,
Lest in this marriage he should be dishonour'd,
Because he married me before to Romeo?
I fear it is, and yet, methinks, it should not,
For he hath still been tried a holy man.
How if, when I am laid into the tomb,
I wake before the time that Romeo
Come to redeem me? there's a fearful point.
Shall I not then be stifled in the vault,
To whose foul mouth no healthsome air breathes in,
And there die strangled ere my Romeo comes?
Or, if I live, is it not very like,
The horrible conceit of death and night,
Together with the terror of the place,
As in a vault, an ancient receptacle,
Where for this many hundred years the bones
Of all my buried ancestors are pack'd,
Where bloody Tybalt, yet but green in earth,
Lies festering in his shroud, where, as they say,
At some hours in the night spirits resort;
Alack, alack, is it not like that I
So early waking, what with loathsome smells
And shrieks like mandrakes' torn out of the earth,
That living mortals hearing them run mad:
O, if I wake, shall I not be distraught,
Environed with all these hideous fears,
And madly play with my forefathers' joints?
And pluck the mangled Tybalt from his shroud?
And, in this rage, with some great kinsman's bone,
As with a club, dash out my desperate brains?
O, look! methinks I see my cousin's ghost
Seeking out Romeo, that did spit his body
Upon a rapier's point: stay, Tybalt, stay!
Romeo, I come! this do I drink to thee.
           She falls upon her bed, within the curtains

Scene IV

Hall in Capulet's house

Enter Lady Capulet and Nurse

Lady Capulet. Hold, take these keys, and fetch more spices,
   nurse.
Nurse. They call for dates and quinces in the pastry.

Enter Capulet

Capulet. Come, stir, stir, stir! the second cock hath crow'd,
   The curfew-bell hath rung, 'tis three o'clock:
   Look to the bak'd meats, good Angelica,
   Spare not for cost.
Nurse.   Go, you cot-quean, go,
   Get you to bed, faith, you'll be sick to-morrow
   For this night's watching.
Capulet. No, not a whit: what! I have watch'd ere now
   All night for lesser cause, and ne'er been sick.
Lady Capulet. Ay, you have been a mouse-hunt in your
   time;
   But I will watch you from such watching now.
                         Exeunt Lady Capulet and Nurse
Capulet. A jealous-hood, a jealous-hood!

*Enter three or four Servingmen, with spits, and logs,
and baskets*

                              Now, fellow,
   What's there?
First Serv. Things for the cook, sir, but I know not what.
Capulet. Make haste, make haste. (*exit First Serv.*) Sirrah,
   fetch drier logs:

Call Peter, he will show thee where they are.

Sec. Serv. I have a head, sir, that will find out logs,
  And never trouble Peter for the matter.

Capulet. Mass, and well said; a merry whoreson, ha!
  Thou shalt be logger-head. (*exit Sec. Serv.*) Good faith,
    'tis day:
  The county will be here with music straight,
  For so he said he would. (*Music within.*) I hear him near.
  Nurse! Wife! What, ho! What, nurse, I say!

Re-enter Nurse

Go waken Juliet, go and trim her up;
I'll go and chat with Paris: hie, make haste,
Make haste: the bridegroom he is come already:
Make haste, I say.   *Exeunt*

Scene V

Juliet's chamber

Enter Nurse

Nurse. Mistress! what, mistress! Juliet! fast, I warrant her,
    she:
  Why, lamb! why, lady! fie, you slug-a-bed!
  Why, love, I say! madam! sweet-heart! why, bride!
  What, not a word? you take your pennyworths now;
  Sleep for a week; for the next night, I warrant,
  The County Paris hath set up his rest
  That you shall rest but little. God forgive me,
  Marry, and amen, how sound is she asleep!
  I needs must wake her. Madam, madam, madam!
  Ay, let the county take you in your bed;
  He'll fright you up, i' faith. Will it not be?
                                    Undraws the curtains
  What, dress'd! and in your clothes! and down again!
  I must needs wake you. Lady! lady! lady!
  Alas, alas! Help, help! my lady's dead!

O, well-a-day, that ever I was born!
Some aqua-vitæ, ho! My lord! my lady!

Enter Lady Capulet

Lady Capulet. What noise is here?
Nurse.   O lamentable day!
Lady Capulet. What is the matter?
Nurse.   Look, look! O heavy day!
Lady Capulet. O me, O me! My child, my only life,
    Revive, look up, or I will die with thee.
    Help, help! call help.

Enter Capulet

Capulet. For shame, bring Juliet forth; her lord is come.
Nurse. She's dead, deceas'd, she's dead; alack the day!
Lady Capulet. Alack the day, she's dead, she's dead, she's
    dead!
Capulet. Ha! let me see her. Out, alas! she's cold;
    Her blood is settled, and her joints are stiff;
    Life and these lips have long been separated.
    Death lies on her like an untimely frost
    Upon the sweetest flower of all the field.
Nurse. O lamentable day!
Lady Capulet.   O woeful time!
Capulet. Death, that hath ta'en her hence to make me wail,
    Ties up my tongue and will not let me speak.

Enter Friar Laurence and Paris, with Musicians

Friar Laurence. Come, is the bride ready to go to church?
Capulet. Ready to go, but never to return.
    O son, the night before thy wedding-day
    Hath death lain with thy bride: see, there she lies,
    Flower as she was, deflowered by him.
    Death is my son-in-law, death is my heir,
    My daughter he hath wedded: I will die,
    And leave him all, life, living, all is Death's.
Paris. Have I thought long to see this morning's face,
    And doth it give me such a sight as this?
Lady Capulet. Accurst, unhappy, wretched, hateful day!

Most miserable hour that e'er time saw
In lasting labour of his pilgrimage!
But one, poor one, one poor and loving child,
But one thing to rejoice and solace in,
And cruel death hath catch'd it from my sight!
Nurse. O woe! O woeful, woeful, woeful day!
Most lamentable day, most woeful day,
That ever, ever, I did yet behold!
O day! O day! O day! O hateful day!
Never was seen so black a day as this:
O woeful day, O woeful day!
Paris. Beguil'd, divorced, wronged, spited, slain!
Most detestable death, by thee beguil'd,
By cruel cruel thee quite overthrown!
O love! O life! not life, but love in death!
Capulet. Despis'd, distressed, hated, martyr'd, kill'd!
Uncomfortable time, why cam'st thou now
To murder, murder our solemnity?
O child! O child! my soul, and not my child!
Dead art thou! Alack, my child is dead;
And with my child my joys are buried!
Friar Laurence. Peace, ho, for shame! confusion's cure lives
not
In these confusions. Heaven and yourself
Had part in this fair maid, now heaven hath all,
And all the better is it for the maid:
Your part in her you could not keep from death;
But heaven keeps his part in eternal life.
The most you sought was her promotion,
For 'twas your heaven she should be advanc'd:
And weep ye now, seeing she is advanc'd
Above the clouds, as high as heaven itself?
O, in this love, you love your child so ill,
That you run mad, seeing that she is well:
She's not well married that lives married long,
But she's best married that dies married young.
Dry up your tears, and stick your rosemary
On this fair corse, and, as the custom is,

In all her best array bear her to church:
For though fond nature bids us all lament,
Yet nature's tears are reason's merriment.
Capulet. All things that we ordained festival,
 Turn from their office to black funeral:
 Our instruments to melancholy bells;
 Our wedding cheer to a sad burial feast;
 Our solemn hymns to sullen dirges change;
 Our bridal flowers serve for a buried corse,
 And all things change them to the contrary.
Friar Laurence. Sir, go you in; and, madam, go with him;
 And go, Sir Paris; every one prepare
 To follow this fair corse unto her grave:
 The heavens do lour upon you for some ill;
 Move them no more by crossing their high will.

> *They all but the Nurse go forth, casting rosemary*
> *on her and shutting the curtains*

First Mus. Faith, we may put up our pipes, and be gone.
Nurse. Honest good fellows, ah, put up, put up;
 For, well you know, this is a pitiful case.   *Exit*
First Mus. Ay, by my troth, the case may be amended.

> *Enter Peter*

Peter. Musicians, O, musicians, 'Heart's ease, Heart's ease:'
 O, an you will have me live, play 'Heart's ease.'
First Mus. Why 'Heart's ease'?
Peter. O, musicians, because my heart itself plays 'My heart
 is full of woe:' O, play me some merry dump, to comfort
 me.
First Mus. Not a dump we; 'tis no time to play now.
Peter. You will not then?
First Mus. No.
Peter. I will then give it you soundly.
First Mus. What will you give us?
Peter. No money, on my faith, but the gleek; I will give you
 the minstrel.
First Mus. Then will I give you the serving-creature.
Peter. Then will I lay the serving-creature's dagger on your

pate. I will carry no crotchets: I'll re you, I'll fa you; do you note me?

First Mus. An you re us and fa us, you note us.

Sec. Mus. Pray you, put up your dagger, and put out your wit.

Peter. Then have at you with my wit! I will dry-beat you with an iron wit, and put up my iron dagger. Answer me like men:

'When griping griefs the heart doth wound
[And doleful dumps the mind oppress,]
Then music with her silver sound'—

why 'silver sound'? why 'music with her silver sound'?— What say you, Simon Catling?

First Mus. Marry, sir, because silver hath a sweet sound.

Peter. Pretty! What say you, Hugh Rebeck?

Sec. Mus. I say, 'silver sound,' because musicians sound for silver.

Peter. Pretty too! What say you, James Soundpost?

Third Mus. Faith, I know not what to say.

Peter. O, I cry you mercy; you are the singer: I will say for you. It is 'music with her silver sound,' because musicians have seldom gold for sounding:

'Then music with her silver sound
With speedy help doth lend redress.'   *Exit*

First Mus. What a pestilent knave is this same!

Sec. Mus. Hang him, Jack! Come, we'll in here; tarry for the mourners, and stay dinner.   *Exeunt*

ACT V

Scene I

Enter Romeo

Romeo. If I may trust the flattering truth of sleep,
My dreams presage some joyful news at hand:
My bosom's lord sits lightly in his throne,
And all this day an unaccustom'd spirit
Lifts me above the ground with cheerful thoughts.
I dreamt my lady came and found me dead—
Strange dream, that gives a dead man leave to think!—
And breath'd such life with kisses in my lips,
That I reviv'd and was an emperor.
{Ah me! how sweet is love itself possess'd,
When but love's shadows are so rich in joy!}

Enter Balthasar, booted

News from Verona, how now, Balthasar,
{Dost thou not bring me letters from the friar?}
How doth my lady? Is my father well?
How fares my Juliet? that I ask again;
If she be well, then nothing can be ill.
Balthasar. Then nothing can be ill, for she is well:
Her body sleeps in Capels' monument,
And her immortal parts with angels dwell.
{I saw her laid low in her kindred's vault,
And presently took post to tell it you:}
O, pardon me for bringing these ill news,
{Since you did leave it for my office, sir.}
Romeo. Is it e'en so? then I defy my stars!
Thou know'st my lodging: get me ink and paper,
And hire post-horses, I will hence to-night.

Balthasar. I do beseech you, sir, have patience:
  Your looks are pale and wild, and do import
  Some misadventure.
Romeo.   Tush, thou art deceiv'd,
  Leave me, and do the thing I bid thee do.
  Hast thou no letters to me from the friar?
Balthasar. No, my good lord.
Romeo.   No matter: get thee gone,
  And hire those horses, I'll be with thee straight.
                                        Exit Balthasar
  Well, Juliet, I will lie with thee to-night.
  Let's see for means:—O mischief, thou art swift
  To enter in the thoughts of desperate men!
  I do remember an apothecary,
  And hereabouts a' dwells, which late I noted,
  In tatter'd weeds, with overwhelming brows,
  Culling of simples; meagre were his looks,
  Sharp misery had worn him to the bones:
  And in his needy shop a tortoise hung,
  An alligator stuff'd, and other skins
  Of ill-shap'd fishes, and about his shelves
  A beggarly account of empty boxes,
  Green earthen pots, bladders and musty seeds,
  Remnants of packthread, and old cakes of roses,
  Were thinly scatter'd, to make up a show.
  Noting this penury, to myself I said,
  An if a man did need a poison now,
  Whose sale is present death in Mantua,
  Here lives a caitiff wretch would sell it him.
  O, this same thought did but forerun my need,
  And this same needy man must sell it me.
  As I remember, this should be the house:
  Being holiday, the beggar's shop is shut.
  What, ho! apothecary!

                    Enter Apothecary

Apothecary.   Who calls so loud?
Romeo. Come hither, man. I see that thou art poor;
  Hold, there is forty ducats: let me have

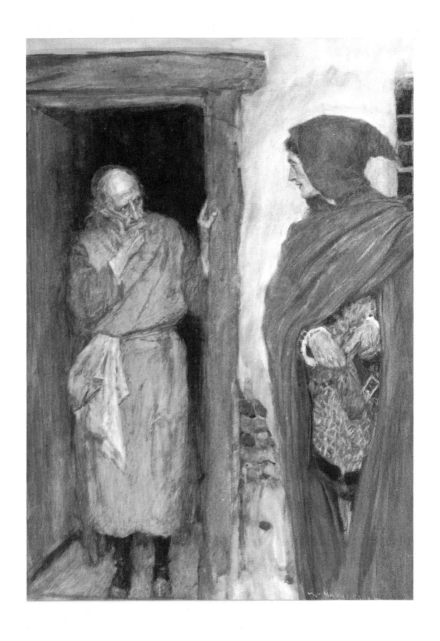

A dram of poison, such soon-speeding gear
As will disperse itself through all the veins,
That the life-weary taker may fall dead,
And that the trunk may be discharg'd of breath
As violently as hasty powder fir'd
Doth hurry from the fatal cannon's womb.
Apothecary. Such mortal drugs I have, but Mantua's law
Is death to any he that utters them.
Romeo. Art thou so bare and full of wretchedness,
And fear'st to die? famine is in thy cheeks,
Need and oppression starveth in thy eyes,
Contempt and beggary hangs upon thy back;
The world is not thy friend, nor the world's law;
The world affords no law to make thee rich;
Then be not poor, but break it, and take this.
Apothecary. My poverty, but not my will, consents.
Romeo. I pay thy poverty and not thy will.
Apothecary. Put this in any liquid thing you will,
And drink it off, and, if you had the strength
Of twenty men, it would dispatch you straight.
Romeo. There is thy gold, worse poison to men's souls,
Doing more murder in this loathsome world,
Than these poor compounds that thou mayst not sell:
I sell thee poison, thou hast sold me none.
Farewell, buy food, and get thyself in flesh.
Come, cordial and not poison, go with me
To Juliet's grave, for there must I use thee. *Exeunt*

Scene II

Friar Laurence's cell

Enter Friar John

Friar John. Holy Franciscan friar! brother, ho!

Enter Friar Laurence

Friar Laurence. This same should be the voice of Friar John.
Welcome from Mantua: what says Romeo?
Or, if his mind be writ, give me his letter.

Friar John. Going to find a bare-foot brother out,
　　One of our order, to associate me,
　　Here in this city visiting the sick,
　　And finding him, the searchers of the town,
　　Suspecting that we both were in a house
　　Where the infectious pestilence did reign,
　　Seal'd up the doors and would not let us forth,
　　So that my speed to Mantua there was stay'd.
Friar Laurence. Who bare my letter then to Romeo?
Friar John. I could not send it,—here it is again,—
　　Nor get a messenger to bring it thee,
　　So fearful were they of infection.
Friar Laurence. Unhappy fortune! by my brotherhood,
　　The letter was not nice, but full of charge
　　Of dear import, and the neglecting it
　　May do much danger. Friar John, go hence;
　　Get me an iron crow and bring it straight
　　Unto my cell.
Friar John. Brother, I'll go and bring it thee.　　　　*Exit*
Friar Laurence. Now must I to the monument alone;
　　Within this three hours will fair Juliet wake:
　　She will beshrew me much that Romeo
　　Hath had no notice of these accidents;
　　But I will write again to Mantua,
　　And keep her at my cell till Romeo come:
　　Poor living corse, clos'd in a dead man's tomb!
　　　　　　　　　　　　　　　　　　　　Exit

Scene III

A churchyard; in it a monument belonging to the Capulets

*Enter Paris and his Page, bearing a torch, flowers,
and sweet water*

Paris. Give me thy torch, boy: hence, and stand aloof:
　　Yet put it out, for I would not be seen.
　　Under yond yew-trees lay thee all along,
　　Holding thine ear close to the hollow ground;
　　So shall no foot upon the churchyard tread,

Being loose, unfirm with digging up of graves,
But thou shalt hear it: whistle then to me,
As signal that thou hear'st some thing approach.
Give me those flowers, do as I bid thee, go.
Page. (*aside*) I am almost afraid to stand alone
Here in the churchyard, yet I will adventure.

Retires

Paris. Sweet flower, with flowers thy bridal bed I strew,—
O woe! thy canopy is dust and stones;—
Which with sweet water nightly I will dew,
Or, wanting that, with tears distill'd by moans:
The obsequies that I for thee will keep
Nightly shall be to strew thy grave and weep.

The Page whistles and calls

The boy gives warning, something doth approach.
What cursed foot wanders this way to-night,
To cross my obsequies and true love's rite?
What, with a torch! Muffle me, night, a while.

Retires

*Enter Romeo and Balthasar, with a torch,
mattock, &c.*

Romeo. Give me that mattock and the wrenching iron.
Hold, take this letter, early in the morning
See thou deliver it to my lord and father.
Give me the light: upon thy life, I charge thee,
Whate'er thou hear'st or seest, stand all aloof,
And do not interrupt me in my course.
Why I descend into this bed of death
Is partly to behold my lady's face,
But chiefly to take thence from her dead finger
A precious ring: a ring that I must use
In dear employment, therefore hence, be gone:
But if thou, jealous, dost return to pry
In what I farther shall intend to do,
By heaven, I will tear thee joint by joint,
And strew this hungry churchyard with thy limbs:
The time and my intents are savage-wild,

More fierce and more inexorable far
Than empty tigers, or the roaring sea.
Balthasar. I will be gone, sir, and not trouble you.
Romeo. So shalt thou show me friendship. Take thou that:
Live, and be prosperous: and farewell, good fellow.
Balthasar. (aside) For all this same, I'll hide me hereabout:
His looks I fear, and his intents I doubt. *Retires*
Romeo. Thou detestable maw, thou womb of death,
Gorg'd with the dearest morsel of the earth:
Thus I enforce thy rotten jaws to open,
And in despite I'll cram thee with more food.

Opens the tomb

Paris. This is that banish'd haughty Montague
That murder'd my love's cousin, with which grief
It is supposed the fair creature died,
And here is come to do some villanous shame
To the dead bodies: I will apprehend him.

Comes forward

Stop thy unhallow'd toil, vile Montague!
Can vengeance be pursued further than death?
Condemned villain, I do apprehend thee,
Obey, and go with me, for thou must die.
Romeo. I must indeed, and therefore came I hither.
Good gentle youth, tempt not a desperate man,
Fly hence and leave me: think upon these gone;
Let them affright thee. I beseech thee, youth,
Put not another sin upon my head,
By urging me to fury: O, be gone!
By heaven, I love thee better than myself,
For I come hither arm'd against myself:
Stay not, be gone, live, and hereafter say,
A madman's mercy bid thee run away.
Paris. I do defy thy conjurations
And apprehend thee for a felon here.
Romeo. Wilt thou provoke me? then have at thee, boy!

They fight

Page. O Lord, they fight! I will go call the watch. *Exit*
Paris. O, I am slain! (*Falls.*) If thou be merciful,
Open the tomb, lay me with Juliet. *Dies*

Romeo. In faith, I will. Let me peruse this face:
  Mercutio's kinsman, noble County Paris!
  What said my man, when my betossed soul
  Did not attend him as we rode? I think
  He told me Paris should have married Juliet:
  Said he not so? or did I dream it so?
  Or am I mad, hearing him talk of Juliet,
  To think it was so? O, give me thy hand,
  One writ with me in sour misfortune's book!
  I'll bury thee in a triumphant grave;
  A grave? O, no, a lantern, slaughter'd youth;
  For here lies Juliet, and her beauty makes
  This vault a feasting presence full of light.
  Death, lie thou there, by a dead man interr'd.
               Laying Paris in the monument
  How oft when men are at the point of death
  Have they been merry! which their keepers call
  A lightning before death: O, how may I
  Call this a lightning? O my love! my wife!
  Death, that hath suck'd the honey of thy breath,
  Hath had no power yet upon thy beauty:
  Thou art not conquer'd, beauty's ensign yet
  Is crimson in thy lips and in thy cheeks,
  And death's pale flag is not advanced there.
  Tybalt, liest thou there in thy bloody sheet?
  O, what more favour can I do to thee
  Than with that hand that cut thy youth in twain
  To sunder his that was thine enemy?
  Forgive me, cousin! Ah, dear Juliet,
  Why art thou yet so fair? shall I believe
  That unsubstantial death is amorous,
  And that the lean abhorred monster keeps
  Thee here in dark to be his paramour?
  For fear of that, I still will stay with thee,
  And never from this palace of dim night
  Depart again: here, here will I remain
  With worms that are thy chamber-maids; O, here
  Will I set up my everlasting rest,
  And shake the yoke of inauspicious stars

From this world-wearied flesh. Eyes, look your last!
Arms, take your last embrace! and, lips, O you
The doors of breath, seal with a righteous kiss
A dateless bargain to engrossing death!
Come, bitter conduct, come, unsavoury guide!
Thou desperate pilot, now at once run on
The dashing rocks thy sea-sick weary bark.
Here's to my love! (*Drinks.*) O true apothecary!
Thy drugs are quick. Thus with a kiss I die.　　*Dies*

Enter, at the other end of the churchyard, Friar Laurence,
with a lantern, crow, and spade

Friar Laurence. Saint Francis be my speed! how oft to-night
　Have my old feet stumbled at graves! Who's there?
Balthasar. Here's one, a friend, and one that knows you well.
Friar Laurence. Bliss be upon you! Tell me, good my friend.
　What torch is yond that vainly lends his light
　To grubs and eyeless skulls? as I discern,
　It burneth in the Capels' monument.
Balthasar. It doth so, holy sir, and there's my master,
　One that you love.
Friar Laurence.　　Who is it?
Balthasar.　　　　　　Romeo.
Friar Laurence. How long hath he been there?
Balthasar.　　　　　　　　Full half an hour.
Friar Laurence. Go with me to the vault.
Balthasar.　　　　　　　　I dare not, sir:
　My master knows not but I am gone hence;
　And fearfully did menace me with death,
　If I did stay to look on his intents.
Friar Laurence. Stay, then; I'll go alone: fear comes upon
　me;
　O, much I fear some ill unlucky thing.
Balthasar. As I did sleep under this yew-tree here,
　I dreamt my master and another fought,
　And that my master slew him.
Friar Laurence.　　　　　Romeo!　　　*Advances*
　Alack, alack, what blood is this, which stains
　The stony entrance of this sepulchre?

What mean these masterless and gory swords
To lie discolour'd by this place of peace?　*Enters the tomb*
Romeo! O, pale! Who else? what, Paris too?
And steep'd in blood? Ah, what an unkind hour
Is guilty of this lamentable chance!
　The lady stirs.　　　　　　　　　　*Juliet wakes*
Juliet. O comfortable friar! where is my lord?
　I do remember well where I should be,
　And there I am: where is my Romeo?　　*Noise within*
Friar Laurence. I hear some noise. Lady, come from that
　　nest
　Of death, contagion and unnatural sleep:
　A greater power than we can contradict
　Hath thwarted our intents: come, come away:
　Thy husband in thy bosom there lies dead;
　And Paris too: come, I'll dispose of thee
　Among a sisterhood of holy nuns:
　Stay not to question, for the watch is coming;
　Come, go, good Juliet; I dare no longer stay.
Juliet. Go, get thee hence, for I will not away.
　　　　　　　　　　　　　　Exit Friar Laurence
　What's here? a cup, clos'd in my true love's hand?
　Poison, I see, hath been his timeless end:
　O churl! drink all, and leave no friendly drop
　To help me after? I will kiss thy lips;
　Haply some poison yet doth hang on them,
　To make me die with a restorative.　　*Kisses him*
　Thy lips are warm.
First Watch. (*within*) Lead, boy: which way?
Juliet. Yea, noise? then I'll be brief. O happy dagger!
　　　　　　　　　　　Snatching Romeo's dagger
　This is thy sheath (*stabs herself*); there rust, and let me
　　die.　　　　　*Falls on Romeo's body, and dies*

　　　　Enter Watch, with the Page of Paris

Page. This is the place, there, where the torch doth burn.
First Watch. The ground is bloody, search about the church-
　　yard:
　Go, some of you, whoe'er you find attach.

Pitiful sight! here lies the county slain;
And Juliet bleeding, warm, and newly dead,
Who here hath lain this two days buried.
Go tell the prince, run to the Capulets,
Raise up the Montagues, some others search:
We see the ground whereon these woes do lie;
But the true ground of all these piteous woes
We cannot without circumstance descry.

Re-enter some of the Watch, with Balthasar

Sec. Watch. Here's Romeo's man, we found him in the
    churchyard.
First Watch. Hold him in safety, till the prince come hither.

Re-enter Friar Laurence, and another Watchman

Third Watch. Here is a friar, that trembles, sighs and weeps:
    We took this mattock and this spade from him,
    As he was coming from this churchyard's side.
First Watch. A great suspicion: stay the friar too.

Enter Prince Escalus and Attendants

Escalus. What misadventure is so early up,
    That calls our person from our morning rest?

Enter Capulet, Lady Capulet, and others

Capulet. What should it be that they so shriek abroad?
Lady Capulet. The people in the street cry Romeo,
    Some Juliet, and some Paris, and all run
    With open outcry toward our monument.
Escalus. What fear is this which startles in our ears?
First Watch. Sovereign, here lies the County Paris slain;
    And Romeo dead, and Juliet, dead before,
    Warm and new-kill'd.
Escalus. Search, seek, and know how this foul murder
    comes.
First Watch. Here is a friar, and slaughter'd Romeo's man,
    With instruments upon them, fit to open
    These dead men's tombs.
Capulet. O heavens! O wife, look how our daughter bleeds!

This dagger hath mista'en, for, lo, his house
Is empty on the back of Montague,
And it mis-sheathed in my daughter's bosom!
Lady Capulet. O me! this sight of death is as a bell
That warns my old age to a sepulchre.

Enter Montague and others

Escalus. Come, Montague, for thou art early up,
To see thy son and heir more early down.
Montague. Alas, my liege, my wife is dead to-night;
Grief of my son's exile hath stopp'd her breath:
What further woe conspires against mine age?
Escalus. Look, and thou shalt see.
Montague. O thou untaught! what manners is in this,
To press before thy father to a grave?
Escalus. Seal up the mouth of outrage for a while,
Till we can clear these ambiguities,
And know their spring, their head, their true descent,
And then will I be general of your woes,
And lead you even to death: meantime forbear,
And let mischance be slave to patience.
Bring forth the parties of suspicion.
Friar Laurence. I am the greatest, able to do least,
Yet most suspected, as the time and place
Doth make against me, of this direful murder;
And here I stand, both to impeach and purge
Myself condemned, and myself excus'd.
Escalus. Then say at once what thou dost know in this.
Friar Laurence. I will be brief, for my short date of breath
Is not so long as is a tedious tale.
Romeo, there dead, was husband to that Juliet;
And she, there dead, that Romeo's faithful wife:
I married them, and their stol'n marriage-day
Was Tybalt's dooms-day, whose untimely death
Banish'd the new-made bridegroom from this city,
For whom, and not for Tybalt, Juliet pin'd.
You, to remove that siege of grief from her,
Betroth'd and would have married her perforce
To County Paris: then comes she to me,

And with wild looks bid me devise some means
To rid her from this second marriage,
Or in my cell there would she kill herself.
Then gave I her (so tutor'd by my art)
A sleeping potion, which so took effect
As I intended, for it wrought on her
The form of death: meantime I writ to Romeo,
That he should hither come, as this dire night,
To help to take her from her borrow'd grave,
Being the time the potion's force should cease.
But he which bore my letter, Friar John,
Was stay'd by accident, and yesternight
Return'd my letter back. Then all alone
At the prefixed hour of her waking
Came I to take her from her kindred's vault,
Meaning to keep her closely at my cell
Till I conveniently could send to Romeo:
But when I came, some minute ere the time
Of her awaking, here untimely lay
The noble Paris and true Romeo dead.
She wakes, and I entreated her come forth,
And bear this work of heaven with patience:
But then a noise did scare me from the tomb,
And she too desperate would not go with me,
But, as it seems, did violence on herself.
All this I know, and to the marriage
Her nurse is privy: and, if aught in this
Miscarried by my fault, let my old life
Be sacrific'd some hour before his time
Unto the rigour of severest law.
Escalus. We still have known thee for a holy man.
Where's Romeo's man? what can he say in this?
Balthasar. I brought my master news of Juliet's death,
And then in post he came from Mantua
To this same place, to this same monument.
This letter he early bid me give his father,
And threaten'd me with death, going in the vault,
If I departed not, and left him there.
Escalus. Give me the letter, I will look on it.

Where is the county's page, that rais'd the watch?
Sirrah, what made your master in this place?
Page. He came with flowers to strew his lady's grave,
  And bid me stand aloof, and so I did:
  Anon comes one with light to ope the tomb,
  And by and by my master drew on him,
  And then I ran away to call the watch.
Escalus. This letter doth make good the friar's words,
  Their course of love, the tidings of her death:
  And here he writes that he did buy a poison
  Of a poor 'pothecary, and therewithal
  Came to this vault, to die and lie with Juliet.
  Where be these enemies? Capulet! Montague!
  See, what a scourge is laid upon your hate,
  That heaven finds means to kill your joys with love,
  And I, for winking at your discords too,
  Have lost a brace of kinsmen: all are punish'd.
Capulet. O brother Montague, give me thy hand,
  This is my daughter's jointure, for no more
  Can I demand.
Montague.   But I can give thee more:
  For I will raise her statue in pure gold;
  That whiles Verona by that name is known,
  There shall no figure at such rate be set
  As that of true and faithful Juliet.
Capulet. As rich shall Romeo by his lady lie;
  Poor sacrifices to our enmity!
Escalus. A glooming peace this morning with it brings;
    The sun for sorrow will not show his head:
  Go hence, to have more talk of these sad things;
    Some shall be pardon'd and some punished:
  For never was a story of more woe
  Than this of Juliet and her Romeo.   *Exeunt*